Laboratory Equipment

Label the pieces of laboratory equipment.

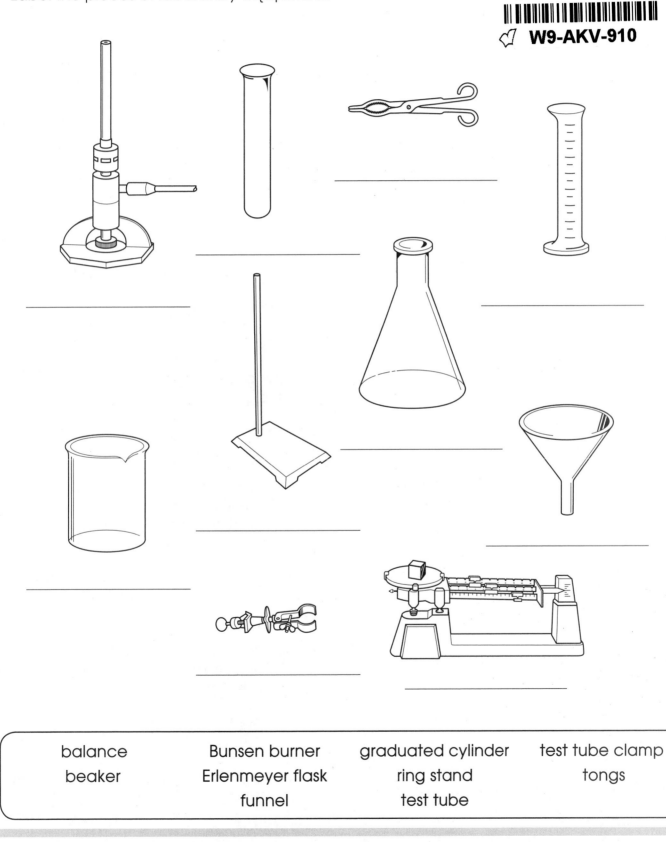

balance	Bunsen burner	graduated cylinder	test tube clamp
beaker	Erlenmeyer flask	ring stand	tongs
	funnel	test tube	

The Scientific Method

Number the steps of the scientific method in the proper order.

_____ Organize and analyze data.

_____ State a hypothesis.

_____ Identify the problem.

_____ State a conclusion.

_____ Design and carry out an experiment.

_____ Make observations and record data.

_____ Gather information.

Match the term with its definition.

1. theory _____

2. law _____

3. hypothesis _____

4. experiment _____

5. variable _____

6. control _____

7. data _____

8. conclusion _____

9. application _____

a. suggested explanation to a problem or observation based upon known information

b. used to test a hypothesis

c. anything that can affect the results of an experiment

d. observations and measurements made during an experiment

e. part within the experiment that is maintained without change to provide a comparison for the part of the experiment containing the variable

f. hypothesis that has been tested and supported by a great amount of evidence over a long period of time

g. statement describing (but not explaining) a natural event or phenomenon

h. new use to which results are put or new technique developed

i. summary that explains whether the data support the hypothesis

Name_____

The Systeme International D'Unites (SI)

The measuring system used in science is the SI, which was adopted according to an international agreement reached in 1960. It is based on the metric system. The standard units in SI are:

Property	Unit	Symbol
mass	kilogram	kg
distance	meter	m
time	second	s
electric current	smpere	A
temperature	Kelvin	K
amount of substance	mole	mol

As with the metric system, the SI utilizes prefixes to change the value of units. The units frequently used in science are:

Prefix	Symbol	Value
mega-	M	1 000 000
kilo-	k	1 000
deci-	d	0.1
centi-	c	0.01
milli-	m	0.001
micro-	μ	0.000 001
nano-	n	0.000 000 0001

Example

How many meters are equivalent to 500 mm?

$$500 \text{ mm} \times \frac{1 \text{ m}}{1,000 \text{ mm}} = 0.5 \text{ m}$$

Make each conversion within the SI.

1. 3.0 m = _____ cm

2. 1,500 mL = _____ L

3. 35 cg = _____ g

4. 0.05 m = _____ mm

5. 2.5 L = _____ mL

6. 0.25 km = _____ m

7. 50,000 μm = _____ m

8. 0.015 g = _____ mg

9. 75 cL = _____ L

10. 2,750 mg = _____ g

What would a reasonable unit use to measure each measurement?

11. distance from earth to moon _____

12. length of a bacterium _____

13. mass of a bowling ball _____

14. mass of an aspirin tablet _____

15. dropperful of medicine _____

Name_____

Self Quiz: Scientific Method and the SI System

Circle the letter of the correct answer.

1. In an experiment, one _____ is tested at a time to determine how it affects results.
    a. control   b. variable   c. problem   d. observation

2. The _____ describes the use of equipment and materials in an experiment.
    a. procedure   b. conclusion   c. control   d. problem

3. A _____ is the part of an experiment that provides a reliable standard for comparison.
    a. procedure   b. theory   c. variable   d. control

4. The information already recorded about a scientific subject is the scientific _____.
    a. record   b. method   c. technique   d. experiment

5. _____ are the recorded facts and measurements from an experiment.
    a. Procedures   b. Data   c. Theories   d. Inferences

6. The practical use of scientific knowledge is called _____.
    a. research   b. inferring   c. procedure   d. technology

7. A _____ is an explanation of observations that have been tested many times.
    a. conclusion   b. hypothesis   c. theory   d. record

8. A(n) _____ is a suggested solution to a scientific problem.
    a. observation   b. hypothesis   c. problem   d. procedure

9. Instruments and our senses are used to make _____ during an experiment.
    a. observations   b. hypotheses   c. problems   d. controls

10. A(n) _____ is performed under carefully controlled conditions to test a hypothesis.
    a. activity   b. observation   c. inference   d. experiment

11. A scientific _____ describes how nature works.
    a. record   b. law   c. hypothesis   d. result

12. To be accepted, a scientific discovery must produce _____ each time it is tested.
    a. the same results b. the same hypothesis c. new conclusions   d. new data

13. If after numerous tests a major hypothesis cannot be shown to be false, it may be accepted as _____.
    a. a control   b. a theory   c. data   d. an observation

14. New observations that do not agree with an accepted theory may cause the theory to be _____.
    a. explained   b. rejected   c. proven   d. recognized

Self Quiz (Continued)

15. A _____ is a logical explanation to a problem based on observation.

    a. control   b. theory   c. conclusion   d. procedure

16. A temperature scale having an abosolute zero below which temperatures do not exist.

    a. Kelvin   b. Celsius   c. Fahrenheit   d. the boiling point

17. The _____ is the unit of time in the SI system.

    a. day   b. second   c. minute   d. hour

18. A _____ is a fixed quantity used for comparison.

    a. procedure   b. variable   c. standard   d. prefix

19. The unit of mass commonly used in the laboratory is the _____.

    a. meter   b. cubic meter   c. gram   d. kilometer

20. The space occupied by an object is its _____.

    a. volume   b. height   c. width   d. length

21. The amount of matter in an object is its _____.

    a. mass   b. volume   c. size   d. balance

22. A scale commonly used by scientists for measuring temperature is the _____ scale.

    a. degree   b. Celsius   c. boiling point   d. Fahrenheit

23. One kilogram has _____.

    a. 0.00 l grams   b. 1,000 milligrams   c. 0.001 milligrams   d. 1,000 grams

24. Standards are important for comparing observations and are used _____.

    a. by everyone   c. only for counting things
    b. only in tropical rain forests   d. only in scientific experiments

25. One-hundredth of a meter is written as a _____.

    a. decimeter   b. millimeter   c. centimeter   d. kilometer

26. How many millimeters make a centimeter?

    a. 100   b. 10   c. 1,000   d. 0.10

27. A prefix meaning one thousand standard units is _____.

    a. milli-   b. centi-   c. kilo-   d. deci-

28. On the Celsius scale, water boils at what temperature?

    a. 32 degrees   b. 212 degrees   c. 0 degrees   d. 100 degrees

29. Which quantity would equal 50 cc of water?

    a. 5,000 mL   b. 500 mL   c. 50 mL   d. 0.5 L

30. Which of the following units would we use to measure the distance to Australia?

    a. millimeters   b. centimeters   c. kilometers   d. kilograms

The Compound Microscope

Label each part on the compound microscope. Describe the purpose or use of each part.

1. base _____

2. mirror _____

3. stage _____

4. arm _____

5. fine adjustment _____

6. coarse adjustment _____

7. ocular/eyepiece _____

8. body tube _____

9. nosepiece _____

10. high power objective _____

11. low power objective _____

12. clip _____

13. diaphragm _____

Microscope Crossword

Across

3. Lens that allows greater magnification

5. Regulates the amount of light

6. The microscope rests on this

10. Used for detailed focusing

11. Eyepiece

12. Platform upon which to mount the slide

13. Holds eyepiece lens at top and objective lens at bottom

14. Holds the tube and stage and attaches them to the base; part by which microscope should be carried

Down

1. Holds the slide in place

2. Lens used to locate the specimen on the slide

4. Used for initial focusing

7. Rotating piece that holds objective lens

8. Reflects light through the stage

9. Chemical sometimes used to make the specimen visible

Name_____

States of Matter

Complete the table by placing a check mark in each column that applies. Then, identify its state as *solid*, *liquid*, or *gas*.

Example	Definite Shape	Definite Volume	Takes Shape of Container	State of Matter
water at 25°C				
ice at -4°C				
steam at 105°C				
iron				
air				
carbon dioxide at 20°C				
juice				
wood				
oil				
nitrogen at room temprature				
milk				
ozone				
glass				
coffee				
chalk				

Name_____

Chemical vs. Physical Change

In a **physical change**, the original substance still exists; it has only changed in form. Energy changes usually only accompany physical changes in phase changes and when substances dissolve. In a **chemical change**, a new substance is produced. Energy changes always accompany chemical changes. Physical changes usually accompany chemical changes.

Classify each situation as a *chemical* or a *physical* change.

1. Sodium chloride dissolves in water. _____

2. Hydrochloric acid reacts with sodium hydroxide to produce a salt, water, and heat. _____

3. A pellet of sodium is sliced in half. _____

4. Water is heated and changes to steam. _____

5. Food is digested. _____

6. Starch molecules are formed from smaller glucose molecules. _____

7. Ice melts. _____

8. Plant leaves lose water through evaporation. _____

9. A red blood cell placed in distilled water swells and bursts. _____

10. The energy in food molecules is transferred into molecules of ATP. _____

11. The roots of a plant absorb water. _____

12. Iron rusts. _____

13. Oxygen is incorporated into hemoglobin to bring it to the cells. _____

14. A person gets cooler by perspiring. _____

15. Proteins are made from amino acids. _____

16. A match burns. _____

17. A toothpick is broken in half. _____

Elements, Compounds, and Mixtures

An **element** consists of only one kind of atom. A **compound** consists of two or more different elements chemically combined in a fixed ratio. A **mixture** can have components in any proportion, and those components are not chemically bound.

Classify each item as an element (*E*), compound (*C*), or mixture (*M*).

1. sodium _____
2. water _____
3. soil _____
4. coffee _____
5. oxygen _____
6. alcohol _____
7. carbon dioxide _____
8. cake batter _____
9. air _____
10. soap _____
11. iron _____
12. salt water _____
13. ice cream _____
14. nitrogen _____
15. eggs _____
16. blood _____
17. table salt _____
18. nail polish _____
19. milk _____
20. cola _____

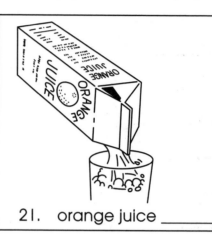

21. orange juice _____

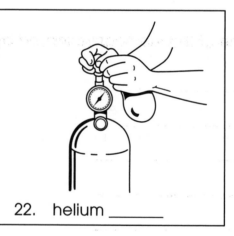

22. helium _____

23. methane _____

Element Symbols

These elements are common in living organisims. Write the symbol for each one.

1. oxygen _____

2. hydrogen _____

3. chlorine _____

4. potassium _____

5. fluorine _____

6. manganese _____

7. carbon _____

8. zinc _____

9. sodium _____

10. sulfur _____

11. phosphorus _____

12. iodine _____

13. magnesium _____

14. nitrogen _____

15. copper _____

16. iron _____

17. calcium _____

18. cobalt _____

Write the name of the element indicated by each symbol.

19. As _____

20. Pb _____

21. Kr _____

22. Ba _____

23. He _____

24. Ne _____

25. Si _____

26. U _____

27. Sn _____

28. Pt _____

29. Rn _____

30. Al _____

31. Cu _____

32. Ag _____

33. Pu _____

34. Sr _____

35. Am _____

36. Au _____

37. Ra _____

38. Ge _____

39. Br _____

40. Hg _____

Parts of the Atom

Using the information provided, determine the number of protons, neutrons, and electrons in each atom. Draw a model of the atom showing the electrons in the proper energy levels.

1. $_1^1H$

    _____ proton

    _____ neutrons

    _____ electron

2. $_6^{12}C$

    _____ protons

    _____ neutrons

    _____ electrons

3. $_{11}^{23}Na$

    _____ protons

    _____ neutrons

    _____ electrons

4. $_{15}^{31}P$

    _____ protons

    _____ neutrons

    _____ electrons

5. $_8^{16}O$

    _____ protons

    _____ neutrons

    _____ electrons

Ionic vs. Covalent Bonds

Nonmetals chemically bond by sharing electrons. The bond is called a **covalent bond**. When an active metal and a nonmetal bond, the active metal transfers one or more electrons to the nonmetal. This bond is called an **ionic bond**. Ionic compounds (except for bases) are also called **salts**.

Classify each compound as *ionic* or *covalent*.

1. $CaCl_2$ _____

2. CO_2 _____

3. H_2O _____

4. $BaCl_2$ _____

5. O_2 _____

6. NaF _____

7. NaS _____

8. S_8 _____

9. SO_3 _____

10. LiBr _____

11. MgO _____

12. C_2H_5OH _____

13. HCl _____

14. N_2 _____

15. NaI _____

16. NO_2 _____

17. Al_2O_3 _____

18. $FeCl_3$ _____

19. P_2O_5 _____

20. N_2O_3 _____

21. H_2 _____

22. K_2O _____

23. KI _____

24. P_4 _____

25. CH_4 _____

26. NaCl _____

Draw an electron shell diagram of the ionic compound calcium oxide, CaO.

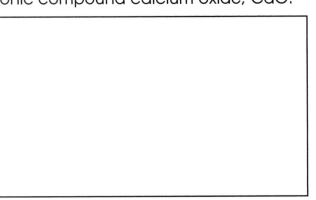

Draw an electron shell diagram of the covalent compound methane, CH_4.

Balancing Equations

Balance each chemical equation.

1. $Na + I_2 \longrightarrow NaI$

2. $N_2 + O_2 \longrightarrow N_2O$

3. $N_2 + H_2 \longrightarrow NH_3$

4. $CH_4 + O_2 \longrightarrow CO_2 + H_2O$

5. $KI + Cl_2 \longrightarrow KCl + I_2$

6. $S + O_2 \longrightarrow SO_3$

7. $H_2O_2 \longrightarrow H_2O + O_2$

8. $Na + H_2O \longrightarrow NaOH + H_2$

9. $H_2O \longrightarrow H_2 + O_2$

10. $KClO_3 \longrightarrow KCl + O_2$

11. $K_3PO_4 + HCl \longrightarrow KCl + H_3PO_4$

12. $CO_2 + H_2O \longrightarrow H_2CO_3$

13. $K_2O + H_2O \longrightarrow KOH$

14. $Mg + HCl \longrightarrow MgCl_2 + H_2$

15. $KOH + H_2SO_4 \longrightarrow K_2SO_4 + H_2O$

Name_____

Self Quiz: Atomic Structure and Equations

Circle the letter of the correct answer.

1. A(n) _____ is a substance made up of one kind of atom.

    a. compound   b. element   c. mixture   d. enzyme

2. The smallest particle of an element having the properties of that element is a(n) _____.

    a. atom   b. compound   c. molecule   d. enzyme

3. A(n) _____ is matter made of substances that are not chemically bonded together.

    a. mixture   b. element   c. compound   d. molecule

4. The correctly written symbol for chlorine is_____.

    a. C   b. CL   c. Ch   d. Cl

5. How many atoms of hydrogen are in each molecule of table sugar, $C_{12}H_{22}O_{11}$?

    a. 11   b. 12   c. 22   d. 45

6. Which of the following is a compound?

    a. iron   b. blood   c. carbon dioxide   d. air

7. A(n) _____ contains two or more atoms bonded together.

    a. mixture   b. molecule   c. atom   d. element

8. A substance that contains two or more different kinds of atoms bonded together is _____.

    a. an element   b. oxygen   c. energy   d. a compound

9. How many atoms of oxygen are represented in the equation: $C + O_2 \rightarrow CO_2$?

    a. 1   b. 2   c. 3   d. 4

10. The smallest part of a compound that still has the properties of that compound is a(n) _____.

    a. atom   b. cell   c. molecule   d. element

11. An atom that contains 15 protons and 10 neutrons within its nucleus will have an atomic mass of _____ amu.

    a. 5   b. 10   c. 15   d. 25

12. An atom of atomic number 12 and mass number 22 contains how many protons?

    a. 10   b. 12   c. 22   d. 34

13. The atom described in problem 12 will have how many electrons?

    a. 10   b. 12   c. 22   d. 34

14. The atom described in problem 12 will have how many neutrons?

    a. 10   b. 12   c. 22   d. 34

15. Elements combine by losing, sharing, or gaining _____.

    a. electrons   b. protons   c. neutrons   d. molecules

Acid, Base, or Salt?

Classify each as an *acid*, a *base*, or a *salt*.

1. HNO_3 _____

2. $NaOH$ _____

3. $NaNO_3$ _____

4. HCl _____

5. KCl _____

6. $Ba(OH)_2$ _____

7. KOH _____

8. H_2S _____

9. $Al(NO_2)_3$ _____

10. H_2SO_4 _____

11. $CaCl_2$ _____

12. H_3PO_4 _____

13. Na_2SO_4 _____

14. $Mg(OH)_2$ _____

15. H_2CO_3 _____

16. NH_4OH _____

17. NH_4Cl _____

18. HBr _____

19. $FeBr_3$ _____

20. HF _____

21. $NaCl$ _____

22. $Ca(OH)_2$ _____

23. $HC_2H_3O_2$ _____

24. $CuCl_2$ _____

25. HNO_2 _____

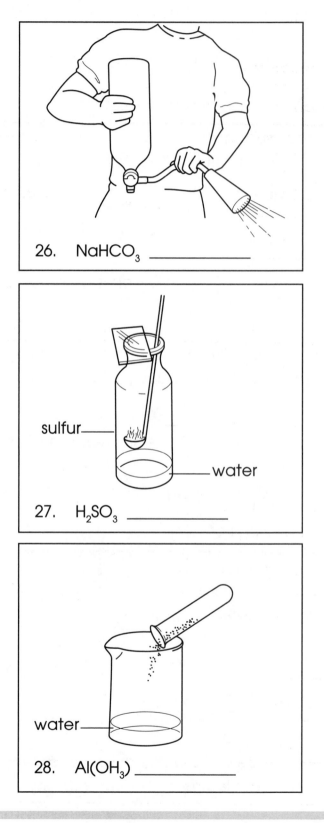

26. $NaHCO_3$ _____

27. H_2SO_3 _____

sulfur

water

28. $Al(OH)_3$ _____

water

pH

pH is a scale that measures the hydronium ion concentration of a solution. A pH of less than 7 indicates an acidic solution. A solution with a pH of 7 is neutral. A solution with a pH of 7 to 14 is basic and contains a higher concentration of hydroxide ions than hydronium ions.

Indicators are substances that change color in the presence of certain ions. Phenolphthalein is colorless in acids and neutral solutions, but pink in a base. Litmus is red in an acid and blue in a base.

For each substance, indicate the pH range expected. Indicate the color the indicator will appear and state the solution's use.

Solution	pH Range	Phenolphtalein	Blue Litmus	Red Litmus	Use
vinegar					
soap					
cola					
ammonia					
rain					
milk					
saliva					
coffee					
gastric juices					
human blood					
orange juice					
drain cleaner					
bleach					
shampoo					

Inorganic vs. Organic Compounds

Matter is often classified as organic or inorganic. Indicate the class for each type of matter as *organic* or *inorganic*. Then, identify its major properties as that of a *salt, acid, base, protein, lipid, nucleic acid,* or *carbohydrate.*

	Matter	Class	Properties of
1.	HCl		
2.	DNA		
3.	starch		
4.	KOH		
5.	sodium chloride		
6.	skin		
7.	animal fat		
8.	glucose		
9.	vegetable oil		
10.	hair		
11.	RNA		
12.	sucrose		
13.	butter		
14.	fingernails		
15.	H_2SO_4		
16.	HNO_3		
17.	gelatin		
18.	molasses		
19.	vinegar		

Dehydration Synthesis

In each example of dehydration synthesis, show how the removal of the water molecule(s) takes place by drawing a box around the components of water. Then, draw the structural formula of each product.

Synthesis of a Fat

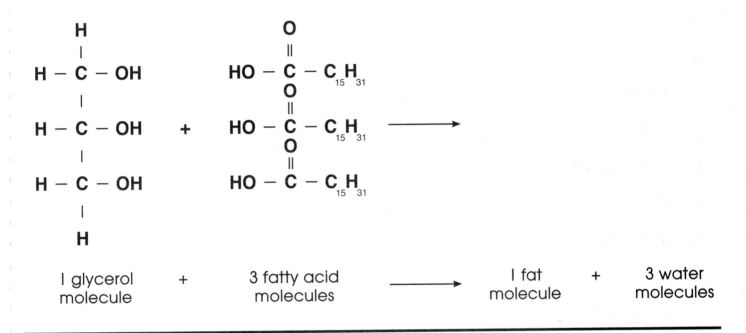

| 1 glycerol molecule | + | 3 fatty acid molecules | ⟶ | 1 fat molecule | + | 3 water molecules |

Formation of a Peptide Bond

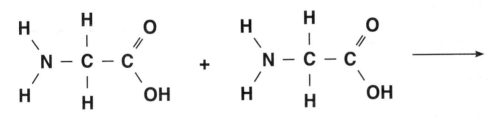

amino acid   +   amino acid   ⟶

dipeptide   +   water

Hydrolysis

Hydrolysis is the opposite of a dehydration synthesis. A large molecule is broken down into two or more smaller molecules by the addition of water.

Draw the structural formulas of the expected products in each hydrolysis reaction.

Breakdown of a Disaccharide to Monosaccharides

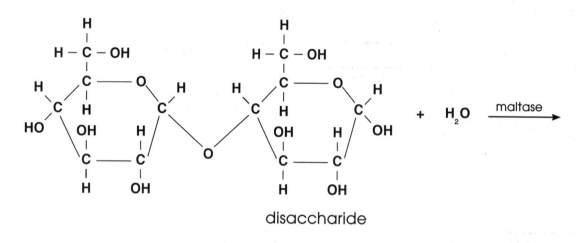

disaccharide

2 monosaccharides

Breakdown of a Lipid

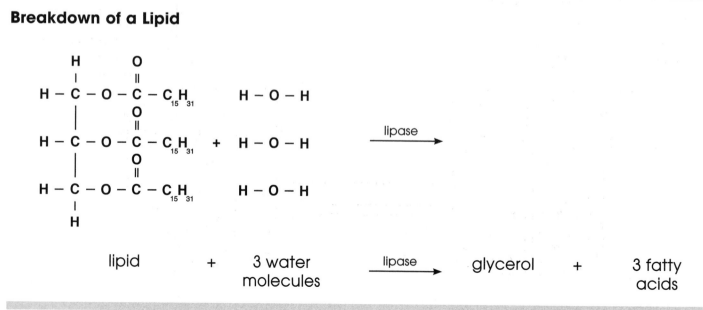

| lipid | + | 3 water molecules | $\xrightarrow{\text{lipase}}$ | glycerol | + | 3 fatty acids |

Diffusion and Osmosis

The diagrams show what each solution would look like after a period of time has passed. Then, label each as *osmosis* or *diffusion*.

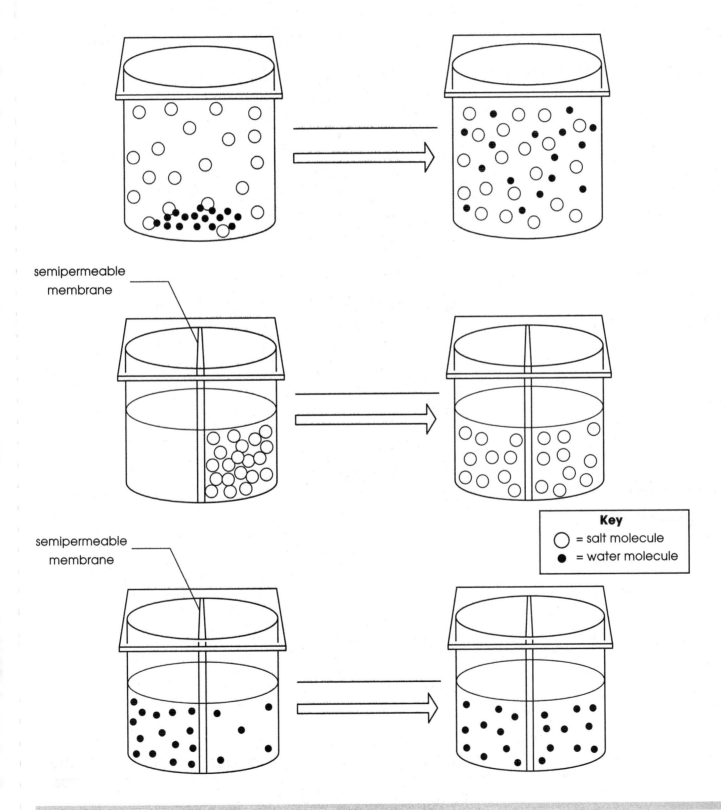

semipermeable membrane

semipermeable membrane

Key

○ = salt molecule

● = water molecule

Animal Cells

Label the organelles in the diagram of a typical animal cell. Describe the function or purpose of each organelle in the cell.

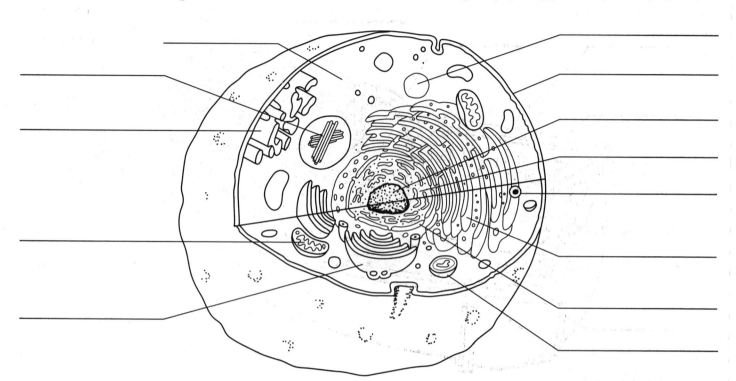

vacuole _____

lysosome _____

ribosome _____

Golgi complex _____

cytoplasm _____

nucleus _____

nucleolus _____

nuclear membrane_____

cell (plasma) membrane _____

mitochondria _____

smooth endoplasmic reticulum _____

rough endoplasmic reticulum _____

centriole _____

Plant Cells

Label the organelles in the diagram of a typical plant cell. Describe the function or purpose of each organelle in the cell.

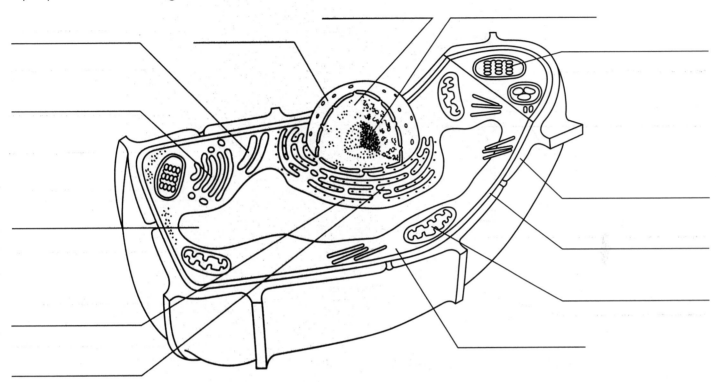

ribosomes _____

Golgi complex _____

cyptoplasm _____

nucleus _____

nucleolus _____

nuclear membrane_____

cell (plasma) membrane _____

mitochondria _____

rough endoplasmic reticulum _____

vacuole _____

cell wall _____

chloroplast _____

smooth endoplasmic reticulum _____

Function of the Organelles

Identify the organelle that performs each function within the cell.

	Function	**Organelle**
1.	Controls the movement into and out of the cell	_____
2.	Watery material that contains many of the materials involved in cell metabolism	_____
3.	Serves as a pathway for the transport of materials throughout the cell; also associated with synthesis and storage	_____
4.	Serves as the control center for cell metabolism and reproduction	_____
5.	Sites of protein synthesis	_____
6.	Involved in the digestion of food within the cell	_____
7.	The "powerhouse" of the cell	_____
8.	Packages and secretes the products of the cell	_____
9.	Involved in cell division in animal cells	_____
10.	Fluid filled organelles enclosed by a membrane; contains stored food or wastes	_____
11.	Site of the production of ribosomes	_____
12.	Controls movement into and out of the nucleus	_____
13.	Gives the cell its shape and provides protection; not found in animal cells	_____
14.	Hairlike structures with the capacity for movement	_____
15.	A long, hairlike structure used for movement	_____
16.	Site of photosynthesis	_____
17.	During cytokinesis, the new cell wall that begins to form in the middle, dividing the two sides	_____
18.	Rod-shaped bodies that carry genetic information	_____

Parts of the Cell

Match each description with the appropriate term.

_____ 1. holds nucleus together

_____ 2. surface for chemical activity

_____ 3. units of heredity

_____ 4. digestion center

_____ 5. where proteins are made

_____ 6. structures involved in mitosis in animal cells

_____ 7. microscopic cylinders that support and give the cell shape

_____ 8. shapes and supports a plant cell

_____ 9. stores and releases chemicals

_____ 10. food for plant cells is made here

_____ 11. spherical body within nucleus

_____ 12. controls entry into and out of cell

_____ 13. traps light and is used to produce food for plants

_____ 14. chromosomes are found here

_____ 15. jellylike substance within cell

_____ 16. contains code that guides all cell activity

_____ 17. minute hole in the nuclear membrane

_____ 18. "powerhouse" of cell

_____ 19. contains water and dissolved minerals

_____ 20. stores food or contains pigment

a.   Golgi bodies

b.   nucleus

c.   chromosomes

d.   vacuole

e.   ribosomes

f.   endoplasmic reticulum

g.   nuclear membrane

h.   centrioles

i.   cytoplasm

j.   chlorophyll

k.   chloroplasts

l.   cell (plasma) membrane

m.   cell wall

n.   mitochondria

o.   lysosome

p.   genes

q.   nuclear pore

r.   nucleolus

s.   plastid

t.   microtubule

Name_____

Cellular Respiration

Complete each sequence.

Glycolysis

glucose + _____ ATP $\xrightarrow{\text{enzymes}}$ 2 _____ + _____ ATP

Anaerobic Respiration

2 pyruvic acid ⟶ 2 _____
      or
2 pyruvic acid ⟶ 2 _____ + 2 _____

Aerobic Respiration

2 pyruvic acid + oxygen $\xrightarrow{\text{enzymes}}$ _____ + _____ + _____ ATP

Complete each sentence.

1. Glycolysis produces a net gain of _____ ATP molecules per molecule of glucose by an anaerobic reaction.

2. Aerobic respiration produces a net gain of _____ ATP molecules per molecule of glucose.

3. _____ respiration is a more efficient producer of energy than anaerobic respiration.

4. The energy contained in a molecule of glucose is changed to a more usable form by combining a _____ atom with _____ to form ATP.

5. When ATP is broken down to _____ and _____ , energy is _____.

6. During glycolysis, glucose is first split into two molecules of _____. This requires the energy released from two molecules of ATP being converted to two molecules of _____.

7. The _____ is then converted to _____ , producing four _____ molecules and two _____ molecules, which are part of the electron transport chain.

8. The _____ transport chain, which supplies the energy needed for the formation of ATP, requires the formation of _____ from NAD^+, and _____ from FAD.

9. The hydrogen necessary in this chain comes from the breaking apart of _____ molecules.

10. The oxygen released is used to form _____.

Stages of Mitosis

Label each diagram of a stage of mitosis in an animal cell with the proper number and name.

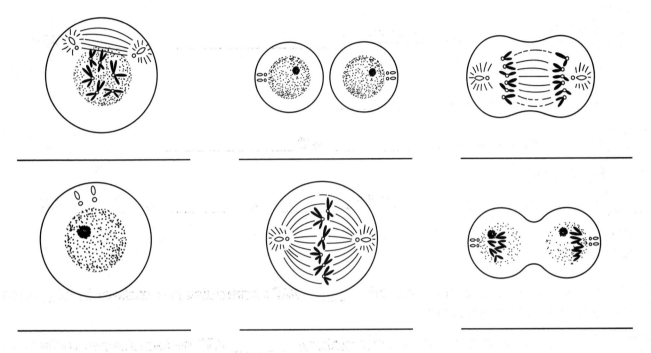

_____   _____   _____

_____   _____   _____

Label each diagram of mitosis in a plant cell with the proper number and name.

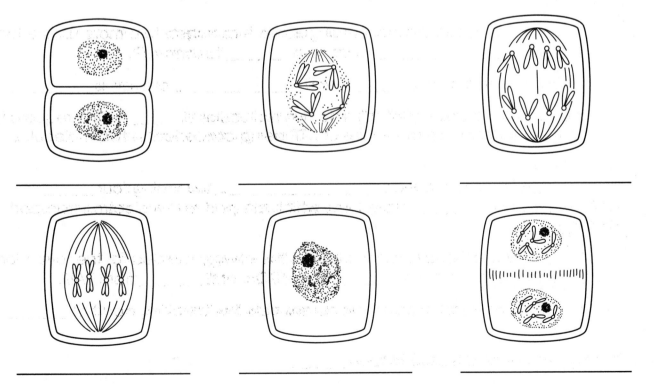

_____   _____   _____

_____   _____   _____

Stages of Meiosis

Number the diagrams of a first meiotic division in the proper order. Label each phase as *prophase I, metaphase I, anaphase I,* or *telophase I.*

_____   _____   _____   _____

Number the diagrams of the second meiotic division. Label each phase as *prophase II, metaphase II, anaphase II,* or *telophase II.*

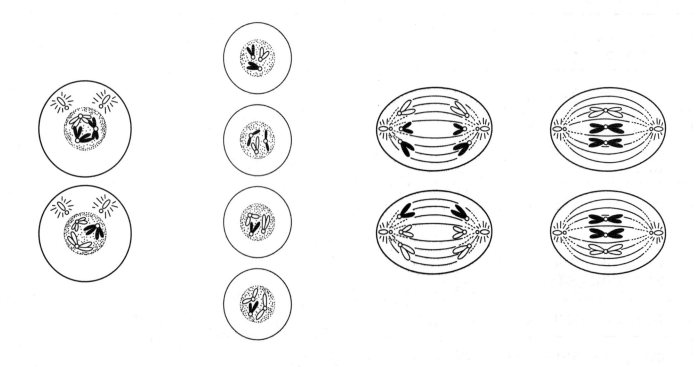

_____   _____   _____   _____

Comparing Mitosis and Meiosis

Determine whether each characteristic applies to mitosis, meiosis, or both by putting a check in the appropriate column(s).

		Mitosis	**Meiosis**
1.	no pairing of homologs occurs		
2.	two divisions		
3.	four daughter cells produced		
4.	associated with growth and asexual reproduction		
5.	associated with sexual reproduction		
6.	one division		
7.	two daughter cells produced		
8.	involves duplication of chromosomes		
9.	chromosome number is maintained		
10.	chromosome number is halved		
11.	crossing over between homologous chromosomes may occur		
12.	daughter cells are identical to parent cell		
13.	daughter cells are not identical to parent cell		
14.	produces gametes		
15.	synopsis occurs in prophase		

Types of Asexual Reproduction

Label the diagrams of types of asexual reproduction as *binary fission*, *budding*, *parthenogenesis*, *regeneration*, *sporulation*, or *vegetative propagation*.

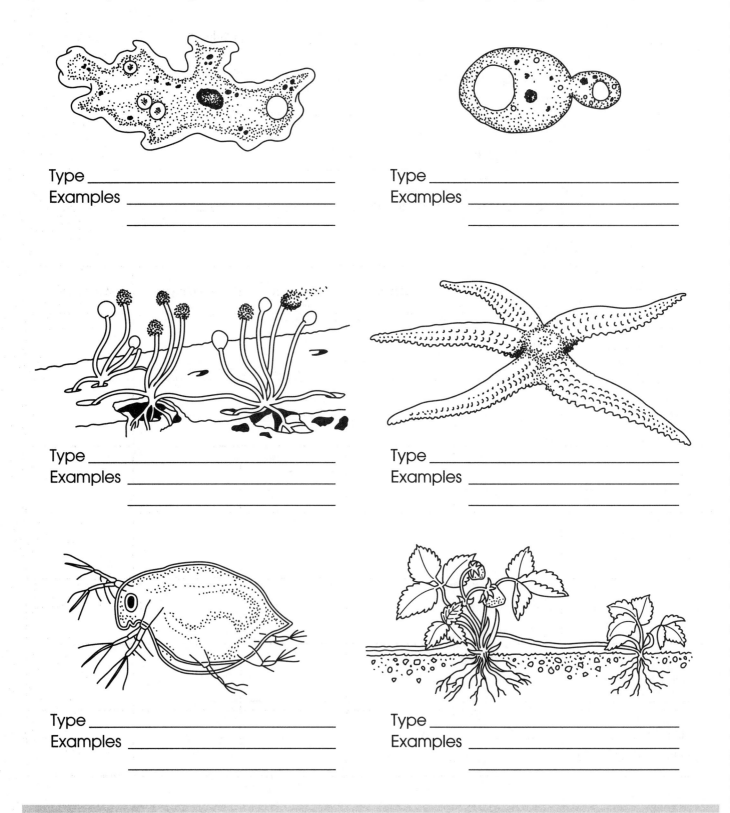

Type _____
Examples _____
_____

Type _____
Examples _____
_____

Type _____
Examples _____
_____

Type _____
Examples _____
_____

Type _____
Examples _____
_____

Type _____
Examples _____
_____

Classification

Number the seven major classification groups in order from the one containing the largest number of organisms to that containing the least.

_____ order   _____ phylum

_____ family   _____ species

_____ kingdom   _____ class

_____ genus

On the chart, classify the five kingdoms according to the characteristics in the left-hand column.

Characteristics	Monera	Protista	Fungi	Plantae	Animalia
cell type (prokaryotic/ eukaryotic)					
number of cells (unicellular/ multicellular)					
cell nucleus (present/absent)					
cell wall (present/absent)					
cell wall composition					
nutrition (autotrophic/ heterotrophic)					
locomotion (present/absent)					

Classifying Organisms

Give the name of each organism and indicate the phylum to which it belongs.

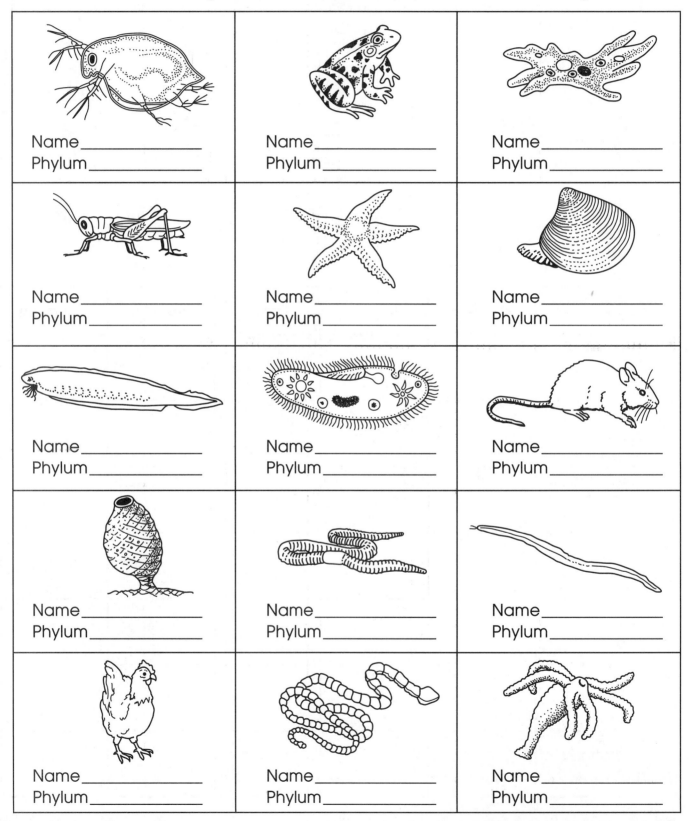

Name_____
Phylum_____

Name_____
Phylum_____

Name_____
Phylum_____

Name_____
Phylum_____

Name_____
Phylum_____

Name_____
Phylum_____

Name_____
Phylum_____

Name_____
Phylum_____

Name_____
Phylum_____

Name_____
Phylum_____

Name_____
Phylum_____

Name_____
Phylum_____

Name_____
Phylum_____

Name_____
Phylum_____

Name_____
Phylum_____

Nutrition in Protozoans

Label the parts on the diagram of an amoeba. State the function or purpose of each part.

a. food vacuole _____

b. pseudopods_____

c. nucleus _____

d. contractile vacuole_____

e. cell membrane _____

f. ectoplasm _____

_____

_____

g. endoplasm_____

_____

_____

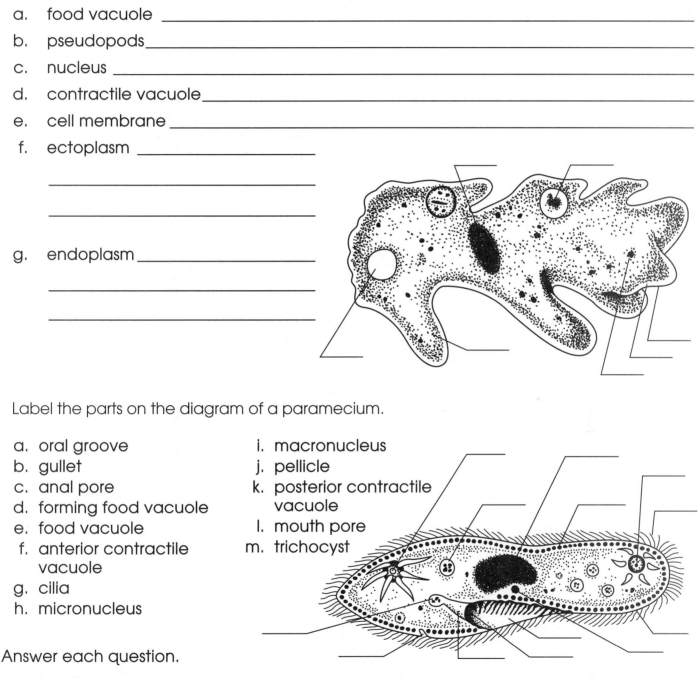

Label the parts on the diagram of a paramecium.

a. oral groove
b. gullet
c. anal pore
d. forming food vacuole
e. food vacuole
f. anterior contractile
    vacuole
g. cilia
h. micronucleus

i. macronucleus
j. pellicle
k. posterior contractile
    vacuole
l. mouth pore
m. trichocyst

Answer each question.

1. Under what conditions does a paramecium discharge its trichocysts?_____

_____

2. How does a paramecium react if it encounters an obstacle?_____

_____

Nutrition in Hydra

Label the parts of the hydra on the diagram. State the function or purpose of each part.

mouth _____

_____

tentacle _____

_____

gastrovascular cavity _____

_____

nematocysts _____

_____

basal disk _____

_____

egg _____

_____

ovary _____

_____

sperm _____

_____

testis _____

_____

bud _____

_____

mesoglea _____

_____

Complete each sentence.

The _____ move food through the _____ into the gastrovascular (digestive) cavity. When the lining of the digestive cavity secretes _____, the food is broken up into tiny pieces. The partly digested food is then engulfed by special cells in the lining that _____ it further. Any undigested or indigestible material is egested through the _____.

Classification and Protists

Match the definition with the correct word. Not all words will be used.

_____ 1. method of sexual reproduction in paramecia

_____ 2. protozoan with short, hairlike structures used for movement

_____ 3. fingerlike projections of cytoplasm

_____ 4. protozoan with a three-stage life cycle

_____ 5. largest category in a kingdom

_____ 6. first word in a scientific name

_____ 7. science of classifying living things

_____ 8. smallest category in a kingdom

_____ 9. division of a class

_____ 10. method of reproduction in an amoeba

a. pseudopod

b. genus

c. conjugation

d. slime mold

e. paramecium

f. order

g. class

h. fission

i. species

j. taxonomy

k. phylum

Match the functions to the correct organelle. Not all words will be used.

_____ 11. gives shape to the paramecium and euglena

_____ 12. controls sexual reproduction in the paramecium

_____ 13. used for excretion of waste _____ products

_____ 14. contains chlorophyll

_____ 15. reacts to light

_____ 16. used for movement by euglena

_____ 17. controls metabolism of a paramecium

_____ 18. used for movement by a paramecium

_____ 19. The paramecium ingests its food through this opening.

a. cilia

b. chloroplast

c. micronucleus

d. oral groove

e. contractile vacuole

f. pellicle

g. flagellum

h. cytostome

i. eyespot

j. pseudopod

k. macronucleus

Name_____

Self Quiz: Classification and Protists

Circle the letter of the correct answer.

1. Of the following groups, a _____ contains animals that are least alike.
   a. family   b. phylum   c. division   d. class

2. Which of the following groupings contain the most closely related organisms?
   a. family   b. phylum   c. genus   d. kingdom

3. Which of the following is a correctly written scientific name?
   a. *Panthera Leo*   b. *panthera leo*   c. *PANTHERA LEO*   d. *Panthera leo*

4. The smallest category of a kingdom is a(n) _____.
   a. division   b. species   c. phylum   d. genus

5. _____ is the science of classifying living things.
   a. Astronomy   b. Biology   c. Taxonomy   d. Zoology

6. The cat and dog belong to the same order but different _____.
   a. kingdoms   b. classes   c. families   d. divisions

7. Living things are usually classified into five _____.
   a. phyla   b. kingdoms   c. classes   d. divisions

8. Which of the following is a *Felis domesticus*?
   a. horse   b. house cat   c. house finch   d. lion

9. What language is used for scientific names?
   a. English   b. Swedish   c. German   d. Latin

10. Organisms are classified into the group with which they share the greatest number of _____.
    a. food   b. territory   c. characteristics   d. time

11. Why does each organism have a specific scientific name?
    a. for study and communication   c. name contains important information
    b. classification is less involved   d. easier to alphabetize all organisms

12. Protozoans and slime molds belong to a group of organisms known as _____.
    a. protists   b. fungi   c. lichens   d. parasites

13. The fingerlike projections of cytoplasm used by some protozoans for movement and obtaining food are:
    a. hyphae   b. sporangia   c. pseudopods   d. oral grooves

14. A protist that has chlorophyll and produces its own food is a(n) _____ protist.
    a. plantlike   b. sporozoan   c. animallike   d. saprophyte

15. A protist covered with many short hairlike structures used for movement is a _____.
    a. parasite   b. ciliate   c. flagellate   d. lichen

16. Which of the following protists have shells made of silica?
    a. diatoms   b. ciliates   c. amoeba   d. paramecia

17. The kingdom with one-celled organisms that are plantlike, animallike, and funguslike is _____.
    a. amoeba   b. protozoa   c. protista   d. fungi

18. The long, hairlike structures protists use for locomotion are _____.
    a. cilia   b. flagella   c. pseudopods   d. trichocysts

Name_____

Self Quiz: Viruses

Complete each sentence.

1. Viruses consist of nucleic acids covered by a coat of _____ .

2. Viruses, unlike bacteria, are not composed of _____ .

3. The only life function viruses can perform is _____ .

4. Protection against some viral diseases can be produced by_____ .

5. Name three viral diseases:_____, _____ and _____ .

6. A vaccine is made from a _____form of the virus.

7. Two natural defenses the body has against viruses are _____

   and _____ .

AIDS	antibodies	cells	interferon
measles	mumps	protein	reproduction
	vaccines	weakened	

Label the *nucleic acid* and *protein coat* in the polyhedral and rod-shaped viruses.
Label the *capsid, collar, tail sheath, tail fiber*, and *base plate* in the bacteriophage.

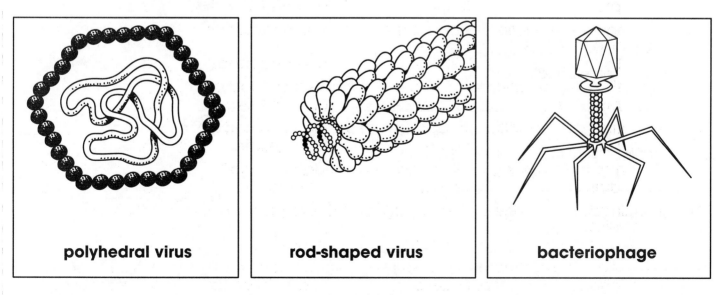

polyhedral virus   **rod-shaped virus**   **bacteriophage**

Bacteria—Typical Monerans

Structure of Bacteria

Label the parts of a moneran on the diagram. State the function or purpose of each.

flagella _____

ribosomes _____

nucleoid _____

cell wall _____

_____

cell (plasma) membrane _____

_____

capsule_____

_____

_____

The diagrams below show **conjugation**, a means of genetic transfer but not reproduction in bacteria. During conjugation, a plasmid is transferred from a donor to a recipient bacterium.

Label the *donor bacterium*, the *recipient bacterium*, the *plasmid*, and the *cytoplasmic bridge* on the diagrams. Then, answer the questions.

1. By what process do bacteria reproduce?

    _____

2. What structure do some bacteria form under unfavorable conditions?

    _____

3. What do the monerans lack in their cell structure that is present in most other organisms?

    _____

4. Are the monerans prokaryotic or eukaryotic?

    _____

Self Quiz: Monerans

Complete each sentence. Not all words will be used.

1. Monerans have no definite _____, but can still carry on reproduction.

2. Monerans have no _____, but can still carry on cellular respiration.

3. Cyanobacteria may also be called _____.

4. When cyanobacterial multiply rapidly in a pond, they use up all of the _____.

5. Bacteria come in three shapes: _____, _____, and _____.

6. Some bacteria have a whiplike tail called a _____.

7. Bacteria that do not need oxygen to live are called _____.

8. Bacteria reproduce by the process of _____.

9. Bacteria that live on dead organic matter are called _____.

10. A relationship between two organisms that does not harm either one is _____.

11. Two conditions bacteria need to live are _____ and _____.

12. Four ways we can control bacterial growth are _____, _____, _____, and _____.

13. _____ are the oldest known and simplest organism.

14. _____ bacteria live in nodules on the roots of plants, fixing atmospheric nitrogen, thus making it available for their own metabolic activities.

15. _____ is the most important source of variability in bacteria.

16. Many scientists have suggested that _____ should be considered a separate kingdom because they are remarkably different from all the bacteria.

17. _____ are the source of over 2,000 kinds of antibiotics.

18. _____ are the causative agents of syphilis and Lyme disease.

actinomycetes	canning	mutation	refrigeration
anaerobes	chemosynthetic	mutualism	rodlike
archaebacteria	cyanobacteria	nitrogen fixing	round
bacteria	flagellum	nucleus	saprophytes
binary fission	freezing	oxygen	spiral
blue-green algae	mitochondria	proper temperature	spirochetes
	moisture	radiation	

Types of Fungi

Label the parts on the diagram of a mushroom.

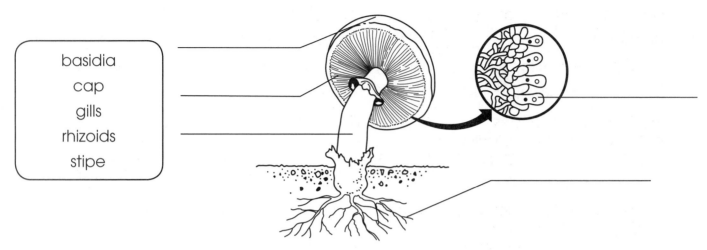

| basidia |
| cap |
| gills |
| rhizoids |
| stipe |

Label the parts on the diagram of bread mold.

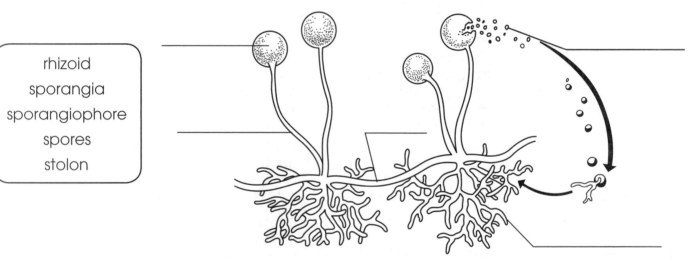

| rhizoid |
| sporangia |
| sporangiophore |
| spores |
| stolon |

Label the parts on the diagram of a yeast cell.

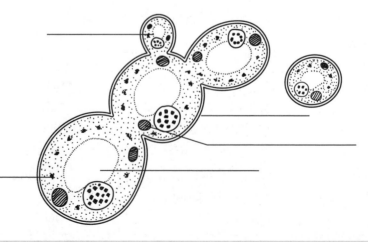

| bud |
| cell wall |
| cytoplasm |
| nucleus |
| vacuole |

Self Quiz: Fungi

Circle the letter of the correct answer.

1. During the process of _____, energy is released.
   a. parasitism   b. fermentation   c. mutualism   d. reproduction
2. _____ are saclike structures that produce many spores.
   a. Pseudopods   b. Gilia   c. Sporangia   d. Hyphae
3. Club fungi produce spores on a sac called a(n) _____.
   a. bud   b. basidium   c. ascus   d. stripe
4. Bread mold produces masses of threadlike structures called_____.
   a. flagella   b. cilia   c. hyphae   d. pseudopods
5. _____ are fungi that produce spores in special structures on the tips of hyphae.
   a. Yeasts   b. Lichens   c. Mushrooms   d. Sporangia fungi
6. _____ is a type of sexual reproduction in which an outgrowth from the parent organism forms a new organism.
   a. Budding   b. Zygospore   c. Sporangia   d. Basidia
7. Sac fungi are fungi that _____.
   a. look like mosses   c. are helpful because they produce enzymes
   b. are one-celled   d. produce spores inside an ascus
8. Yeast cells may reproduce by forming spores or by _____.
   a. fermentation b. budding   c. respiration   d. dehydration
9. A sporangium fungus obtains food by _____.
   a. respiration   b. dehydration   c. absorption   d. mutualism
10. Club fungi include puffballs, bracken fungi, and _____.
    a. molds   b. yeasts   c. mushrooms   d. lichens
11. A sporangium fungus reproduces by _____.
    a. budding and spores   c. anaerobic respiration
    b. spores and zygospores   d. a micronucleus
12. Unlike a plant, a fungus does not have _____.
    a. very many cells   b. chlorophyll
    c. cell walls   d. buds
13. Which one of the following helpful fungi is used to flavor cheese?
    a. mushrooms   b. saprophytic fungi   c. yeast   d. molds
14. Each basidium will produce how many spores?
    a. thousands   b. hundreds   c. four   d. ten
15. The basidia are found on what part of the mushroom?
    a. stipe   b. gills   c. cap   d. hyphae
16. Fermentation produces what products?
    a. alcohol and carbon dioxide   c. alcohol and water
    b. air bubbles and sugar   d. carbon dioxide and sugar
17. Masses of hyphae are called _____.
    a. basidia   b. sporangia   c. mycelium   d. asci
18. Another name for anaerobic respiration in fungi is _____.
    a. budding   b. reproduction   c. breathing   d. fermentation
19. A person who studies fungi is called a_____.
    a. fungicide   b. mycologist   c. zygospore   d. saprophyte
20. The cell walls of fungi are made of _____.
    a. cellulose   b. chitin   c. silica   d. tissue

Autotrophs vs. Heterotrophs

An **autotroph** is an organism that is capable of forming organic compounds from inorganic compounds in its environment. In other words, an autotroph can make its own food. **Heterotrophs** must get their food from other organisms.

Classify each organism as an autotroph (*A*) or a heterotroph (*H*).

1. maple tree _____
2. human _____
3. wheat _____
4. fungi _____
5. amoeba _____
6. green algae _____
7. house fly _____
8. fern _____
9. dandelion _____
10. goldfish _____

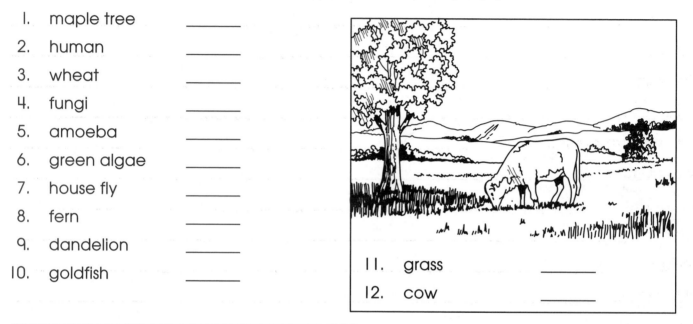

11. grass _____
12. cow _____

Most autotrophic nutrition is a result of photosynthesis. Heterotrophic nutrition involves the taking in and processing of food and the elimination of wastes.

Classify each process as related primarily to autotrophic nutrition (*A*) or heterotrophic nutrition (*H*).

13. chlorophyll _____
14. digestion _____
15. phagocytosis _____
16. photolysis _____
17. rhizoids _____
18. lipase _____
19. carbon fixation _____
20. pseudopods _____
21. PGAL _____
22. light reaction _____

23. maltose _____
24. CO_2 is used _____
25. ingestion _____
26. chloroplasts _____
27. dark reaction _____
28. grana _____
29. proteose _____
30. glucose production _____
31. stroma _____
32. bile _____

Name_____

Cross Section of a Leaf

Label the parts of the leaf in the diagram. Give the purpose or function of each part.

lower epidermis _____

upper epidermis _____

palisade layer _____

cuticle _____

stomata _____

guard cells _____

vein (fibrovascular bundle) _____

spongy layer _____

air space _____

xylem _____

phloem _____

chloroplasts _____

mesophyll _____

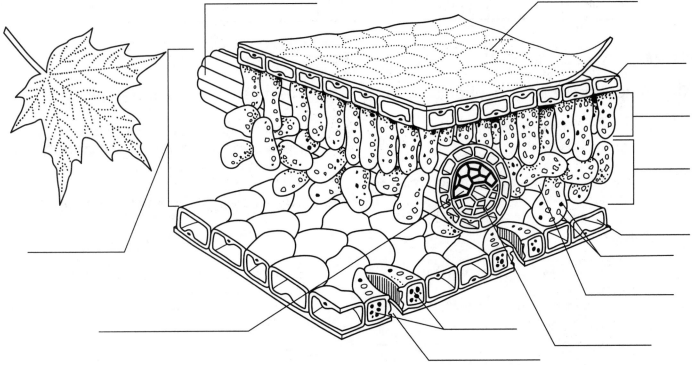

Name_____

Leaf Crossword

Across

3. Outermost cellular layer of the leaf

5. Where most photosynthesis takes place in the leaf

8. Carry food and water to the cells

10. Food-making process occurring in leaves

11. Gas necessary for photosynthesis

12. Green pigment necessary for photosynthesis

Down

1. Control the size of the stoma opening

2. Allow the exchange of gases between the environment and the air spaces inside the leaf

4. Organelles that contain chlorophyll

6. Beneath the palisade layer

7. End product of photosynthesis

9. Waxy coat of the leaf

Structure of a Root

Label the parts on the diagrams of a cross section and longitudinal section of a root.

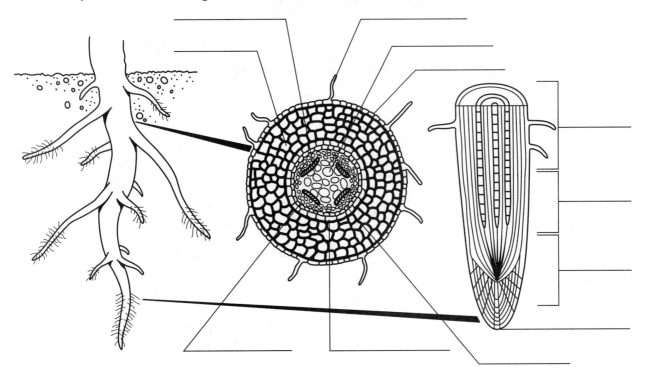

cambium	pericycle	region of meristematic growth
cortex	phloem	root cap
epidermis	region of differentiation	vascular cylinder
foot hair	region of elongation	xylem

Complete each sentence.

The end of the root that absorbs minerals and _____ is the_____.

The root tip is protected by several layers of cells called the _____. In the

region of _____, cells mature and become specialized in function. Some cells

in the outer layer develop_____. These _____ are elongated cells

that increase the surface area of the root to maximize absorption of _____

and minerals from the _____. The _____ and vascular cylinder

are separated by the _____. In the vascular cylinder, the xylem and

_____ are separated by the _____.

Structure of a Flower

Label the parts of a flower in the diagram. Give the purpose or function of each part.

ovary _____

style _____

stigma _____

sepal _____

receptacle _____

pedicel _____

petal _____

filament _____

anther _____

pollen grain _____

_____

pistil _____

_____

stamen _____

_____

ovule _____

_____

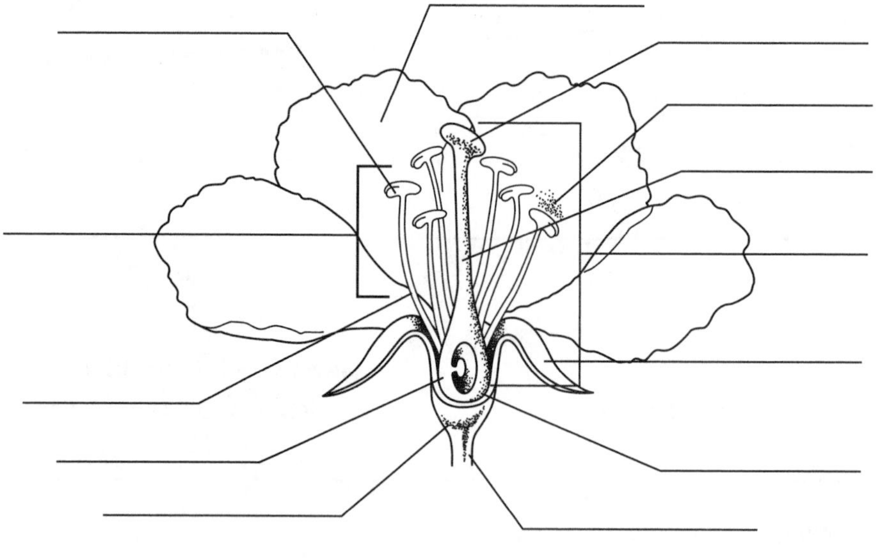

Complete each sentence.

For more flowers to grow, _____ must take place. In pollination,

pollen is transferred from the _____ to the _____. In detail,

pollen is transferred from the _____ of the stamen to the _____

of the pistil. In some flowers, pollen falls on the stigma of the _____ flower;

_____-pollination occurs. In other flowers, pollen from _____ flower

falls on the stigma of a _____ flower; _____-pollination takes place.

Structure of the Stamen and Pollen

Label the parts on the diagrams of double fertilization in a flower.

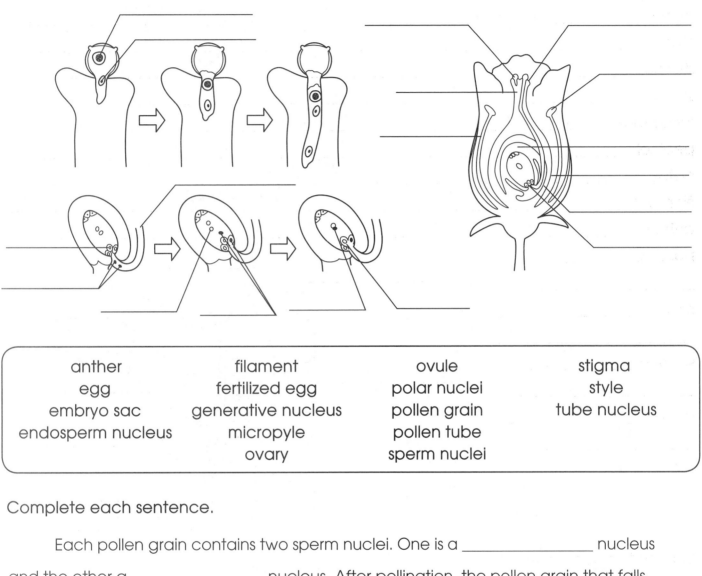

anther	filament	ovule	stigma
egg	fertilized egg	polar nuclei	style
embryo sac	generative nucleus	pollen grain	tube nucleus
endosperm nucleus	micropyle	pollen tube	
	ovary	sperm nuclei	

Complete each sentence.

Each pollen grain contains two sperm nuclei. One is a _____ nucleus and the other a _____ nucleus. After pollination, the pollen grain that falls on the _____ begins to form a _____, under the control of the _____ nucleus. The pollen tube grows through the _____ into the ovary. The _____ nucleus moves down the _____ where it divides into _____ sperm nuclei. Inside the embryo sac, one _____ nucleus joins with the _____ nucleus, producing a fertilized _____. This is _____. The second _____ nucleus joins with the _____ nuclei to form an _____ nucleus, which develops into the _____.

Name_____

Ecological Relationships

Use the food web to answer each question.

1. When the hawk is the third-order consumer, the number of second-order consumers shown is_____.

2. The food chain that includes insect-eating birds is _____ _____.

3. The animal that consumes the largest number of different types of first-order and second-order consumers is the _____.

4. All of the animals that are herbivores are _____ consumers.

5. If no snakes were in the food web, the squirrels and rabbits could still be eaten by the _____.

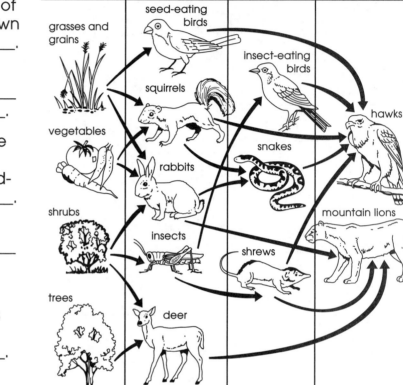

Producers   First-Order Consumers   Second-Order Consumers   Third-Order Consumers

grasses and grains · seed-eating birds · squirrels · insect-eating birds · vegetables · rabbits · snakes · hawks · shrubs · insects · shrews · mountain lions · trees · deer

Complete each sentence.

6. A group of independent organisms in a particular environment is a(n) _____.

7. Organisms that break down dead tissue are _____.

8. All of the living and nonliving things in a selected area form a(n) _____.

9. The particular environment to which a species is adapted is its_____.

10. The special role and place of an organism within its habitat is its _____.

11. An animal that eats both plants and animals is a(n) _____.

12. Members of a single species that occupy a common area form a(n) _____.

13. Animals that feed only on dead organisms are _____.

community	habitat	population
decomposers	niche	scavengers
ecosystem	omnivore	

Punnett Squares—One Trait

In a certain species of animal, black fur (B) is dominant over brown fur (b). Using the following Punnett square, predict the genotypes and phenotypes of the offspring whose parents are both Bb, or have heterozygous black fur.

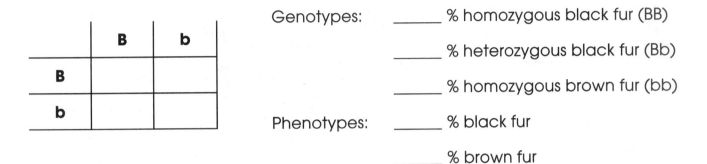

Genotypes: _____ % homozygous black fur (BB)

_____ % heterozygous black fur (Bb)

_____ % homozygous brown fur (bb)

Phenotypes: _____ % black fur

_____ % brown fur

Now, do the same when one parent is homozygous black and the other is homozygous brown.

Genotypes: _____ % homozygous black fur (BB)

_____ % heterozygous black fur (Bb)

_____ % homozygous brown fur (bb)

Phenotypes: _____ % black fur

_____ % brown fur

Repeat the process again when one parent is heterozygous black and the other is homozygous brown.

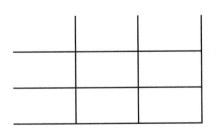

Genotypes: _____ % homozygous black fur (BB)

_____ % heterozygous black fur (Bb)

_____ % homozygous brown fur (bb)

Phenotypes: _____ % black fur

_____ % brown fur

Blood Type and Inheritance

In blood typing, the gene for type A and the gene for type B are codominant. The gene for type O is recessive. Using Punnett squares, determine the possible blood types of the offspring when:

1. Father is type O, Mother is type O

    _____ % O

    _____ % A

    _____ % B

    _____ % AB

2. Father is type A, homozygous; Mother is type B, homozygous

    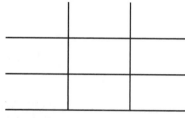

    _____ % O

    _____ % A

    _____ % B

    _____ % AB

3. Father is type A, heterozygous; Mother is type B, heterozygous

    _____ % O

    _____ % A

    _____ % B

    _____ % AB

4. Father is type O, Mother is type AB

    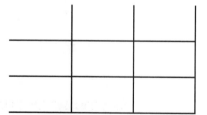

    _____ % O

    _____ % A

    _____ % B

    _____ % AB

5. Father and Mother are both type AB

    _____ % O

    _____ % A

    _____ % B

    _____ % AB

Punnett Squares—Two Traits

In a **dihybrid cross**, when two traits are considered, the number of possible combinations in the offspring increases.

Suppose that black hair (B) is dominant over blond hair (b) and brown eyes (E) are dominant over blue eyes (e). What percent of offspring could be expected to have blond hair and blue eyes if:

the father has black hair (heterozygous) and brown eyes (heterozygous) and the mother has blond hair and blue eyes?

Genotype of father—BbEe
Genotype of mother—bbee

	BE	Be		
be				

_____ % blond hair and blue eyes

both parents have black hair (heterozygous) and brown eyes (heterozygous)?

Genotype of father—_____
Genotype of Mother—_____

_____ % blond hair and blue eyes

In each dihybrid cross, the phenotype ratio of individuals with brown hair and brown eyes, brown hair and blue eyes, blond hair and brown eyes, and blond hair and blue eyes is _____:_____:_____:_____.

Human Pedigrees

By studying a human pedigree, you can determine whether a trait is dominant or recessive. Use the key to interpret the three pedigrees. Remember, the individual with the trait could be homozygous dominant or heterozygous dominant.

A. The pedigree shows the inheritance of attached earlobes for four generations.

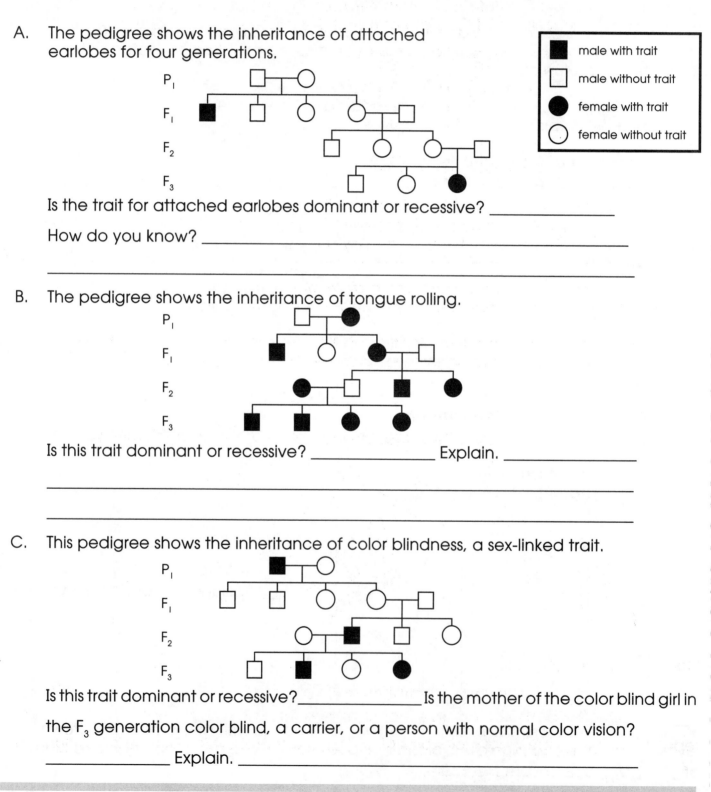

Key
- ■ male with trait
- □ male without trait
- ● female with trait
- ○ female without trait

Is the trait for attached earlobes dominant or recessive? _____

How do you know? _____

_____

B. The pedigree shows the inheritance of tongue rolling.

Is this trait dominant or recessive? _____ Explain. _____

_____

_____

C. This pedigree shows the inheritance of color blindness, a sex-linked trait.

Is this trait dominant or recessive?_____ Is the mother of the color blind girl in

the F$_3$ generation color blind, a carrier, or a person with normal color vision?

_____ Explain. _____

Name_____

DNA Molecule and Replication

The building blocks of the DNA molecule are **nucleotides**, which consist of a phosphate, a deoxyribose sugar, and a nitrogenous base.

The letters representing the four different nitrogeneous bases are shown in the nucleotides in the diagram. Place the name of the base next to its letter symbol.

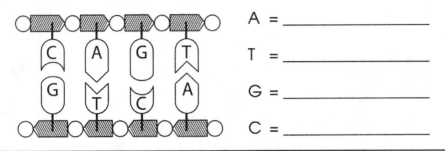

A = _____

T = _____

G = _____

C = _____

The DNA molecule has a double helix shape. Two strands of DNA are coiled around each other and attached by bonds between the nitrogenous bases of each chain. Adenine always bonds with thymine, and cytosine always bonds with guanine.

In the illustration, label a *phosphate* and a *deoxyribose sugar*. Fill in the symbol for each base depending on its complementary base in the opposite strand.

The second diagram shows the replication of DNA. Fill in the symbol for each base. Label the *original strand*, a *new strand*, and a *free-floating nucleotide*.

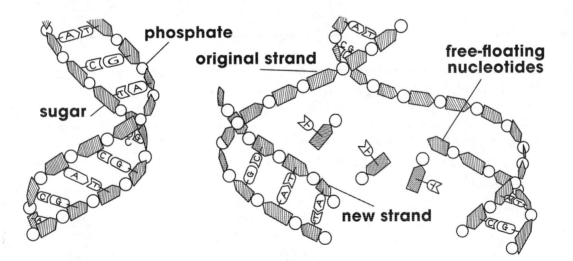

Complete each sentence.

The credit for discovery of the structure of DNA was given to _____ and

_____. The shape of the DNA molecule is described as a _____. After

replication, _____ identical molecules of _____ are produced. A gene is a sequence

of _____ in a DNA molecule.

mRNA and Transcription

Transcription

Fill in the blanks. On the illustration of transcription, label the *DNA*, the *newly forming mRNA*, the *completed strand of mRNA*, and a *free nucleotide*.

Messenger RNA (mRNA) carries the instructions to make a particular _____ of the DNA from the _____ to the ribosomes. The process of producing mRNA from instructions in the DNA is called _____. During transcription, the DNA molecule unwinds and separates, exposing the nitrogenous bases. Free RNA _____ pair with the exposed bases. No _____ (T) is in RNA. _____ (U) pairs with adenine (A) instead. RNA contains the sugar _____ instead of deoxyribose. The mRNA molecule is completed by the formation of _____ between the RNA _____, and it then separates from the DNA. The mRNA molecule is a _____ strand, unlike DNA.

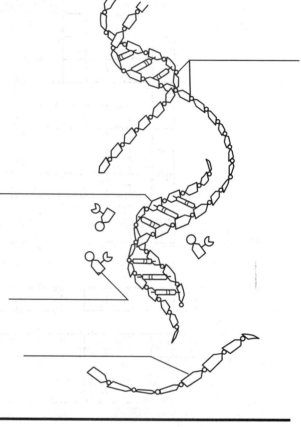

Codons

Each combination of three nitrogenous bases on the mRNA molecule is a **codon**, a three letter code word for a specific amino acid.

The table shows the mRNA codon for each amino acid. Use the table to answer each question.

1. The codon for trytophan is _____.

2. Leucine has _____ different codons.

3. The codon GAU is for _____.

4. In a stop codon, if the second based is G, the first and third bases are _____ and _____.

		Second Base in Code Word				
		A	**G**	**U**	**C**	
First Base in Code Word	**A**	Lysine	Arginine	Isoleucine	Threonine	**A**
		Lysine	Arginine	Methionine	Threonine	**G**
		Asparagine	Serine	Isoleucine	Threonine	**U**
		Asparagine	Serine	Isoleucine	Threonine	**C**
	G	Glutamic Acid	Glycine	Valine	Alanine	**A**
		Glutamic Acid	Glycine	Valine	Alanine	**G**
		Aspartic Acid	Glycine	Valine	Alanine	**U**
		Aspartic Acid	Glycine	Valine	Alanine	**C**
	U	"Stop" codon	"Stop" codon	Leucine	Serine	**A**
		"Stop" codon	Trytophan	Leucine	Serine	**G**
		Tyrosine	Cysteine	Phenylalanine	Serine	**U**
		Tyrosine	Cysteine	Phenylalanine	Serine	**C**
	C	Glutamine	Arginine	Leucine	Proline	**A**
		Glutamine	Arginine	Leucine	Proline	**G**
		Histidine	Arginine	Leucine	Proline	**U**
		Histidine	Arginine	Leucine	Proline	**C**

© Carson-Dellosa • CD-104643

Genetics Crossword

Across

1. Occurs when a segment of chromosome breaks off and becomes reattached to another chromosome
4. Heterozygous for two traits
7. Humans have 46 _____.
8. Capacity of an allele to suppress the expression of a recessive gene
10. Diagram used to predict the results of genetic crosses
11. This base is found in RNA, but not in DNA
12. Genetic makeup of an individual
16. The assembly of a protein molecule from mRNA
17. The sugar in RNA
18. Found on chromosomes, they determine specific characteristics of the organism
19. Different form of a gene
20. The process of producing mRNA from instructions in DNA
21. The sugar in DNA

Down

2. Occurs when both alleles are equally dominant
3. Subunit of DNA consisting of a nitrogenous base, a sugar, and a phosphate group
5. Double helix in which the genetic code is found
6. Two dominant or two recessive genes for the same trait
9. Process by which DNA makes an exact copy of itself
10. Appearance of an individual due to its genetic makeup
13. Presence of complete extra sets of chromosomes
14. Conducted experiments on heredity in pea plants
15. Site of protein synthesis

Name_____

Life Activities and Body Systems

Match each life activity with its example.

1. nutrition _____
2. circulation _____
3. respiration _____
4. excretion _____
5. synthesis _____
6. regulation _____
7. growth _____
8. reproduction _____
9. metabolism _____
10. homeostasis _____
11. digestion _____

a. a cat has a litter of six kittens

b. the cells utilize glucose to produce energy

c. a plant absorbs minerals from the soil

d. a plant forms large starch molecules from smaller sugar molecules

e. the bloodstream brings oxygen and food to the cells

f. waste products are eliminated during perspiration

g. a person sweats to keep body temperature at a safe level

h. the brain coordinates the various systems of the body

i. process by which food is changed into a form the body can use

j. the human body produces hormones, vitamins, proteins, enzymes, etc. to keep it functioning

k. a 7-pound baby becomes a 180-pound man

Complete each sentence.

The lungs are the main organ of the _____ system, but they are also an organ in the _____ system. The lymph and the lymphatics are part of the _____ system. Although food does not pass through the liver and gallbladder, they are part of the _____ system. As a duct gland, the pancreas is part of the _____ system. As a ductless gland, the pancreas is part of the _____ system. The hypothalamus, through its neurosecretory cells, coordinates the activities of the _____ and _____ systems.

Name_____

Life Activities Crossword

Across

1. Process of producing more organisms to continue the species
5. Information acquired by chemical stimuli or response to the environment that is directed to the brain
6. A chemical messenger that is produced in one part of an organism and triggers a reaction in another part of the organism
7. Response of the body to invasion of foreign substances
11. The organism's actions as a result of sensory, neural, and hormonal factors in response to changes in external or internal conditions
14. The ingestion of food for energy and to provide vitamins and minerals the body cannot make for itself
15. The breakdown of foods into molecules the body can use
16. Distribution of materials within an organism

Down

1. The utilization of oxygen and release of carbon dioxide
2. System that relays commands to skeletal muscles and stimulates glands and other muscle so the organism may continue to live and respond to stimuli
3. Ability to independently move about from place to place
4. Series of changes, beginning with conception, an organism undergoes until the adult stage is reached
8. The sum of all chemical processes within a living cell or organism
9. The homeostatic state of water in an organism
10. The transport of material from one place to another within an organism through the use of internal fluid
12. An organism's increase in size or number of cells, with no developmental changes
13. Control and coordination of all of the activities of an organism

The Frog

Digestive System

Label the parts of a frog's digestive system.

anus
cloaca
esophagus
gallbladder
large intestine
liver
mouth
pancreas
small intestine
stomach

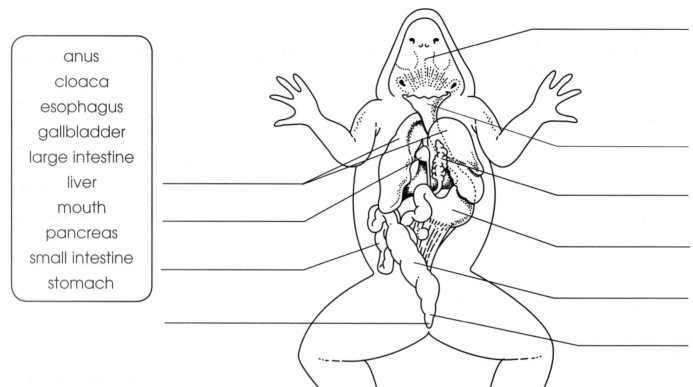

Skeletal System

Label the parts of a frog's skeletal system.

ankle bone
bones of feet
breastbone
collarbone
femur
humerus
knee
pelvic girdle
radio-ulna
shoulder blade
skull
tibio-fibula
vertebrae

The Frog

Nervous System
Label the parts of a frog's nervous system.

brachial nerve
cerebellum
cerebrum
chain of autonomic
ganglia
cranial nerves
medulla oblongata
olfactory lobe
optic lobe
sciatic nerve
spinal cord
spinal nerves

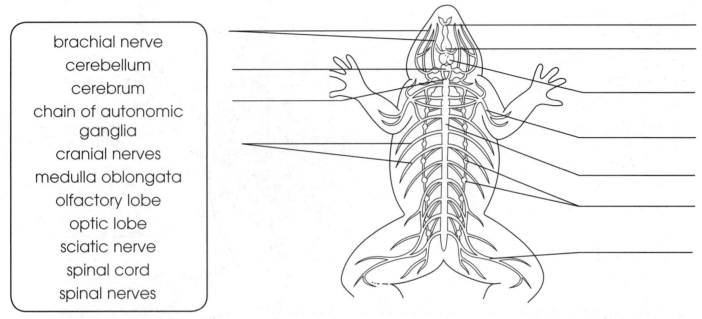

Circulatory System
Label the parts of a frog's circulatory system.

artery to head
artery to leg
left atrium
pulmonary artery
right atrium
vein from head
vein from leg
ventricle

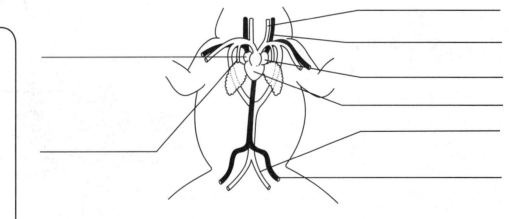

Complete each sentence.

The nervous system of the frog consists of the _____, _____, and nerves. The _____ lobes lie at the anterior end of the brain. Behind these are the lobes of the _____. Next are the _____ lobes, behind which are the _____ and _____. The heart of a frog has _____ventricle. Blood flows from the left _____ to the ventricle, around the body and back to the _____ atrium. From there, it flows to the _____ and then to the left _____.

The Frog

Urinary System
Label the parts of a female frog's urinary system.

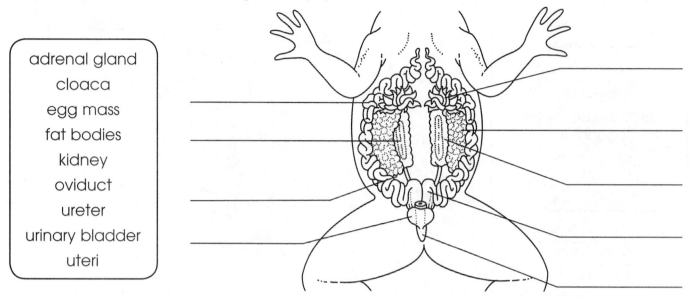

adrenal gland
cloaca
egg mass
fat bodies
kidney
oviduct
ureter
urinary bladder
uteri

Reproductive System
Label the parts of a female frog's reproductive system.

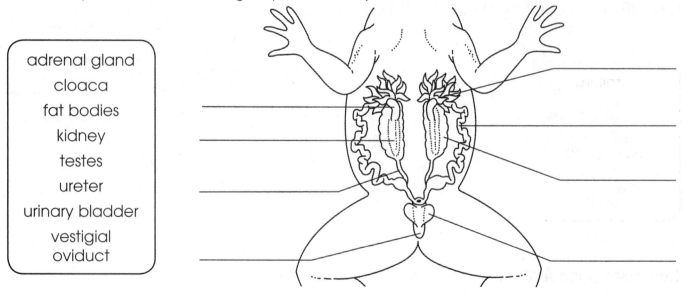

adrenal gland
cloaca
fat bodies
kidney
testes
ureter
urinary bladder
vestigial
oviduct

Complete each sentence.

In the spring the female's _____ become large with _____. When

the eggs are laid, they travel through the _____ into the _____. The male

deposits _____, which are produced in the _____ and travel out the

_____ and over the _____ as they are being laid in the water.

The Earthworm

Digestive System

Label the parts of an earthworm's digestive system.

anus
crop
esophagus
gizzard
intestine
mouth

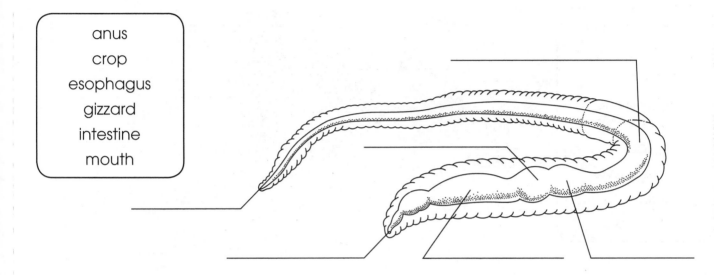

Reproductive System

Label the parts of an earthworm's reproductive system.

clitellum
ovary
sperm receptacle
sperm resevoir
testis

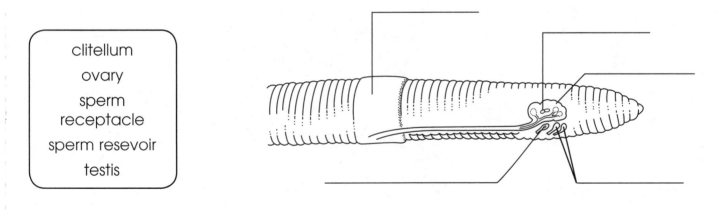

Complete each sentence.

After food enters the mouth, it passes through the _____ and is then stored in the _____. From there, it passes to the _____, where it is mechanically broken down by grinding. After this, it is chemically broken down in the_____. Undigested material is egested through the _____. Since an earthworm produces both eggs and sperm, it is considered to be a _____. However, an earthworm _____ self-fertilize.

The Grasshopper

External Anatomy

Label the parts of a grasshopper's external anatomy. **Use brackets to indicate the three regions of the body: head, thorax, and abdomen.**

antenna

compound eye

ear

egg-laying apparatus

legs

simple eye

spiracles

wings

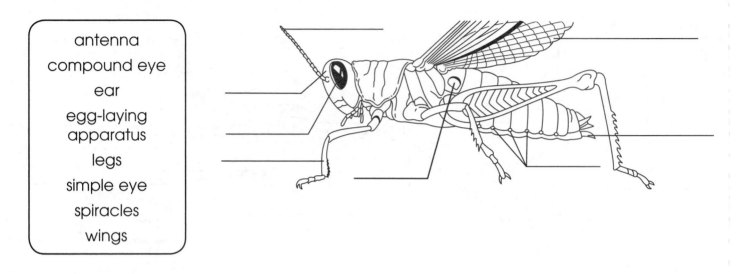

Digestive System

Label the parts of a grasshopper's digestive system.

anus

crop

gastric caeca

gizzard

intestine

mouth

rectum

salivary glands

stomach

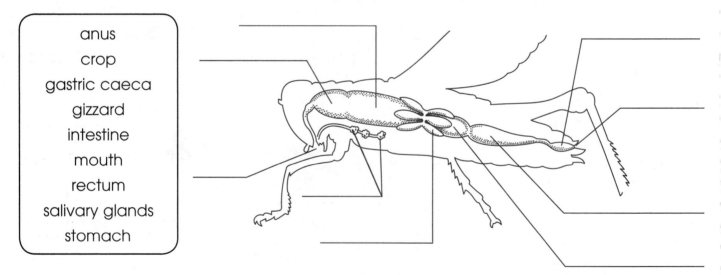

Complete each sentence.

The grasshopper ingests food through the _____. The food is temporarily stored in the _____, after which it passes to the _____ for mechanical grinding. Digestion takes place in the _____ and _____. Undigested waste is egested through the _____. On its thorax, a grasshopper has _____ pairs of _____ legs and _____ pairs of wings. The _____ on the abdomen are used to carry oxygen.

Circulatory Systems of the Earthworm and Grasshopper

Label the parts of an earthworm's circulatory system.

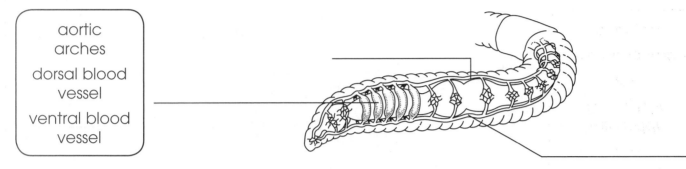

aortic arches

dorsal blood vessel

ventral blood vessel

Label the parts of a grasshopper's circulatory system.

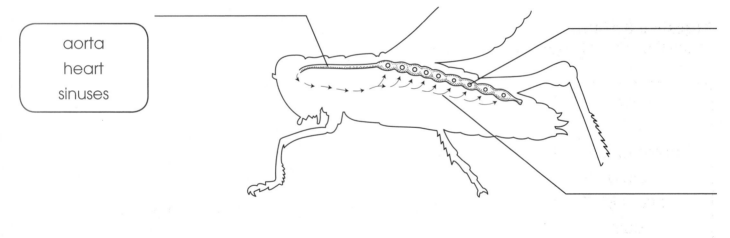

aorta

heart

sinuses

Complete each sentence.

1. Which organism has an open circulatory system?_____

2. Which organism has a closed circulatory system?_____

3. Which type of blood vessel is the aorta? _____

4. In the earthworm, the aortic arches act as _____.

5. In the earthworm, blood flows from the _____ blood vessel to the _____ blood vessel.

6. In a grasshopper, blood re-enters the heart through several pairs of ostia, or _____ .

Name_____

Nervous Systems of the Earthworm and Grasshopper

Label the parts of an earthworm's nervous system.

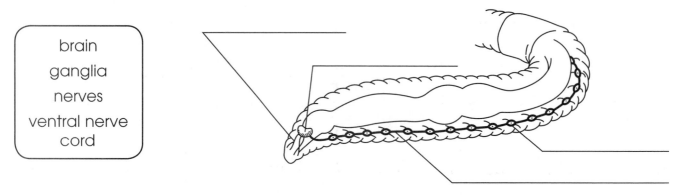

brain
ganglia
nerves
ventral nerve cord

Label the parts of a grasshopper's nervous system.

antennae
brain
compound eye
ganglia
nerves
ventral nerve cord

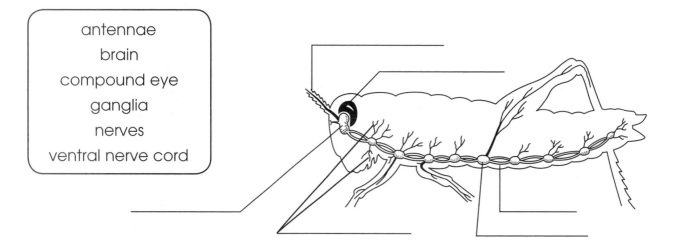

Complete each sentence.

In the earthworm, two nerves from the paired _____ run around each side of the_____ to the _____ side of the worm. Here they join to become a double _____ cord that runs to the last segment. In each _____, they join to become an enlarged _____.

In the grasshopper, the most prominent parts of the brain are the _____ lobes. The large _____ eyes are made up of many _____ so the grasshopper can see in many directions at the same time. The _____ nerve cord contains many _____. The largest ganglion sends messages to the _____ legs.

Gas Exchange in Living Organisms

Complete each sentence.

1. In the simplest organisms, where the outer membrane of the organism is in direct contact with the environment, the exchange of gases occurs by the process of _____.

2. In plants, the exchange of gases occur mainly through the _____ and _____.

3. In the hydra, gas exchange occurs directly between the water and the cells through the process of _____.

4. In the earthworm, the exchange of gases occurs through the _____.

5. Label the parts of a grasshopper's respiratory system.

air sacs
spiracles
tracheal tubes

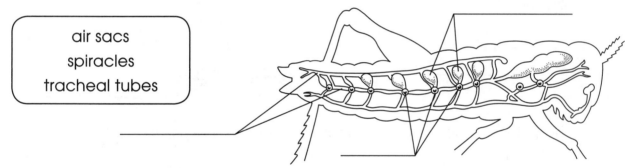

6. Label the parts of a frog's respiratory system.

lungs
mouth
nostrils
skin

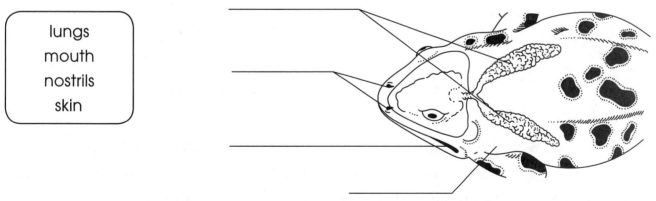

7. Openings in the grasshopper's body by which gases enter and leave are the _____.

8. These openings are attached to _____, which deliver and receive gases at the moist membranes of the animal's internal tissues.

© Carson-Dellosa • CD-104643

65

Excretion in Living Organisms

Complete each sentence.

1. In one-celled organisms and plants, excess water or toxic substances can be contained in _____. Specialized types of these organelles, called _____ _____, can expel these substances from the cell.

2. In the hydra, metabolic waste products are discharged directly into the _____. Gases are also exchanged between the cells and the _____.

3. Label the following parts of an earthworm's excretory system.

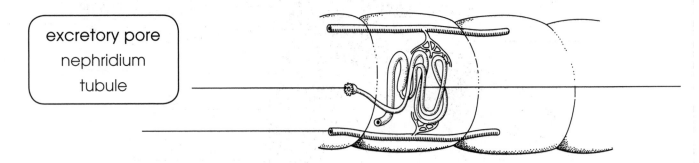

excretory pore
nephridium
tubule

4. Label the following parts of a grasshopper's excretory system.

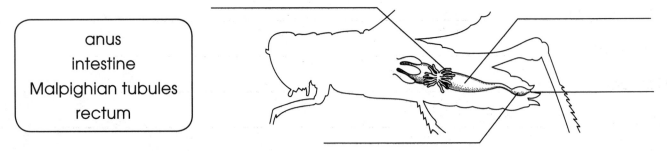

anus
intestine
Malpighian tubules
rectum

Complete each sentence.

In the earthworm, water, mineral salts, and urea are filtered out of the body fluids into the _____ and are then excreted. There are _____ nephridia in most of the body segments. Each nephridium does the same job as the _____ in a human. The sites in the grasshopper in which water, mineral salts, and uric acid accumulate are called _____. These tubules remove cell wastes from the _____ and pass them into the _____. From here they are eliminated from the body along with the _____ wastes.

Structure of a Starfish

Label the parts of a starfish. Give the purpose or function of each part.

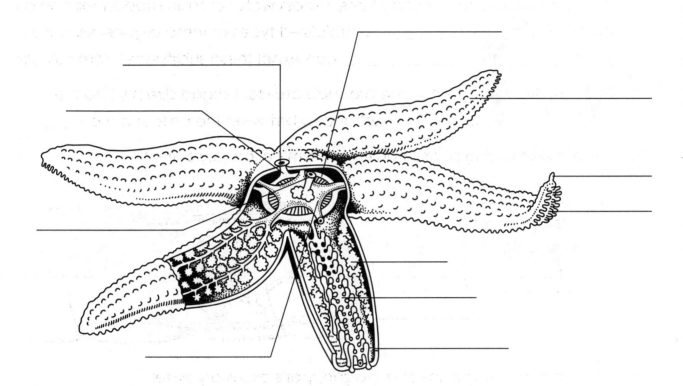

arm _____

sieve plate _____

stomach _____

anus _____

tube feet _____

ring canal _____

stone canal _____

radial canal _____

ampulla _____

gonad _____

eyespot_____

Name_____

Structure of a Crayfish

Label the parts of a crayfish.

abdomen	carapace	swimmerets
antenna	cephalothorax	telson
antennule	cheliped	uropod
anus	compound eye	walking legs
	mandible	

Complete each sentence.

Crayfish seize their food with their _____. The _____ and

_____ crush and chew the food. The _____ are the excretory

organs. The _____ are used for respiration. The "brain" consists of a pair

of _____. Two large nerves extend from the _____ around the

esophagus and join the _____ nerve cord.

Structure of a Bony Fish

Label the parts of a fish.

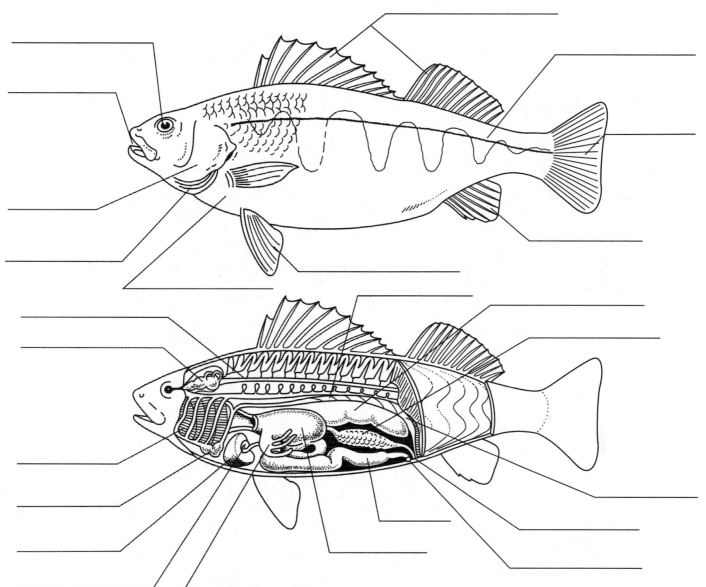

anal fin	gills	liver	pyloric caeca
anus	gill filaments	mouth	spinal cord
brain	heart	operculum	stomach
caudal fin	intestine	ovary/testis	swim bladder
dorsal fins	kidney	pectoral fin	urinary bladder
eye	lateral line	pelvic fin	urogenital opening
gallbladder			

Internal Structure of a Bird

Label the parts of a bird's internal structure.

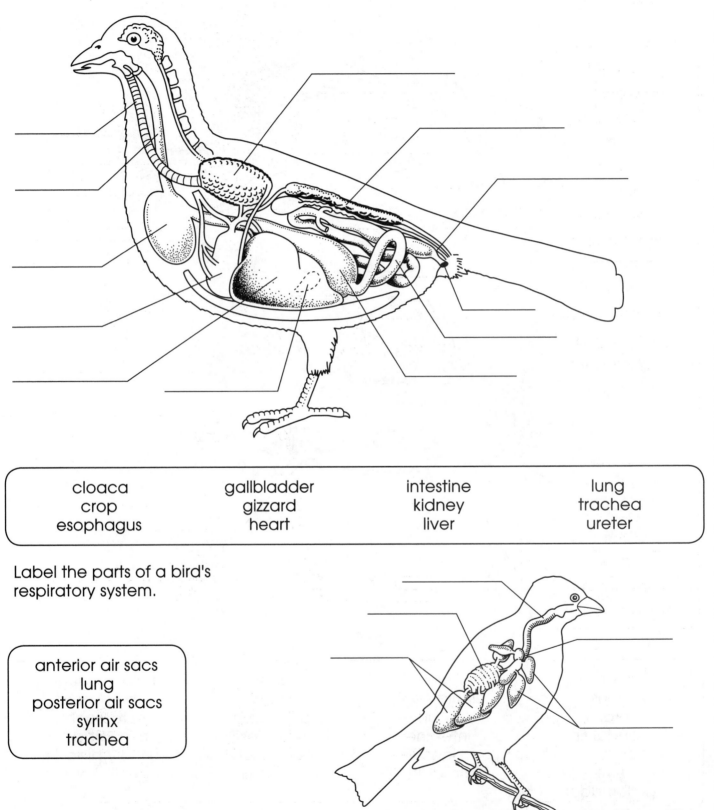

cloaca	gallbladder	intestine	lung
crop	gizzard	kidney	trachea
esophagus	heart	liver	ureter

Label the parts of a bird's respiratory system.

anterior air sacs
lung
posterior air sacs
syrinx
trachea

The Human Skeletal System

Label the parts of a human's skeletal system. Then, label each of the four types of movable joints.

carpals
clavicle
cranium
femur
fibula
humerus
mandible
metacarpals
metatarsals
patella
pectoral girdle
pelvic girdle
phalanges
radius
ribs
scapula
skull
sternum
tarsals
tibia
ulna
vertebrae
vertebral column

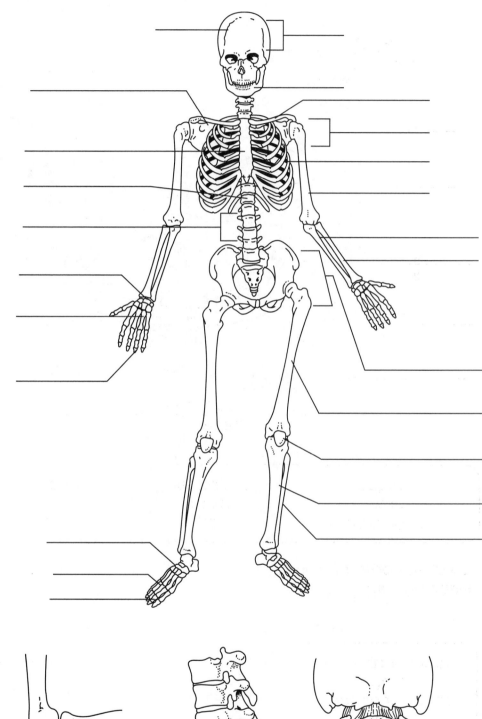

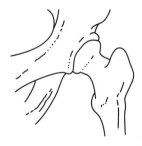

_____   _____   _____   _____

Name_____

Structure of Bones

Label the parts of a long bone on both diagrams. The diagram at the right shows a longitudinal section; the other, a cross section.

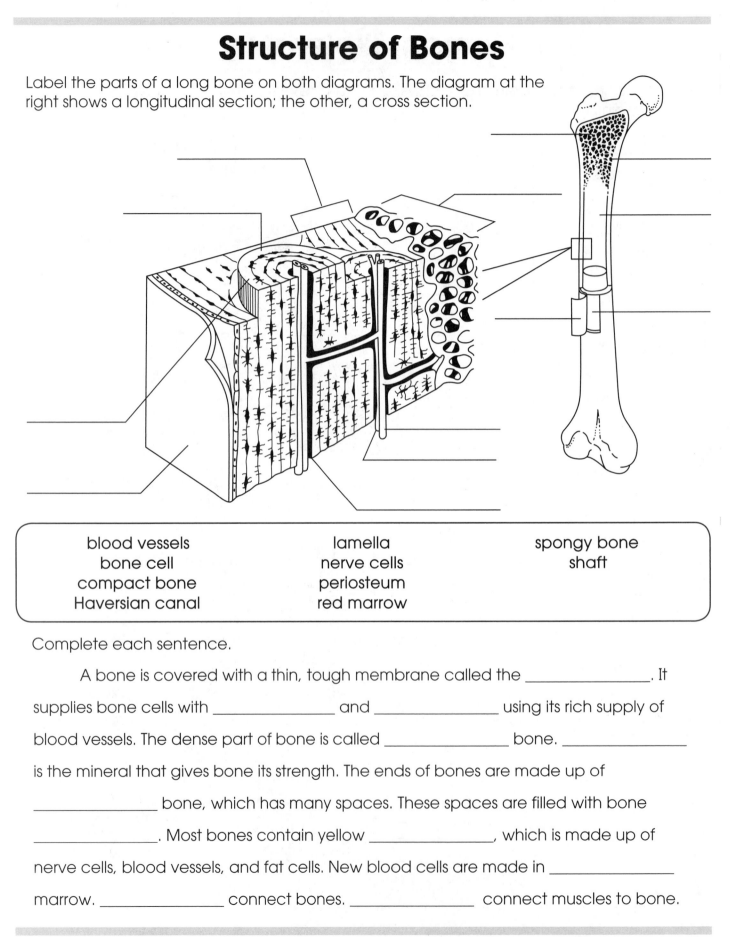

blood vessels	lamella	spongy bone
bone cell	nerve cells	shaft
compact bone	periosteum	
Haversian canal	red marrow	

Complete each sentence.

A bone is covered with a thin, tough membrane called the _____. It supplies bone cells with _____ and _____ using its rich supply of blood vessels. The dense part of bone is called _____ bone. _____ is the mineral that gives bone its strength. The ends of bones are made up of _____ bone, which has many spaces. These spaces are filled with bone _____. Most bones contain yellow _____, which is made up of nerve cells, blood vessels, and fat cells. New blood cells are made in _____ marrow. _____ connect bones. _____ connect muscles to bone.

© Carson-Dellosa • CD-104643

Name_____

Human Skin

Label the parts of human skin.

capillary
dermis
epidermis
erector muscle
fat cells
hair
hair follicle
nerve ending
pore
sweat gland
subcutaneous tissue

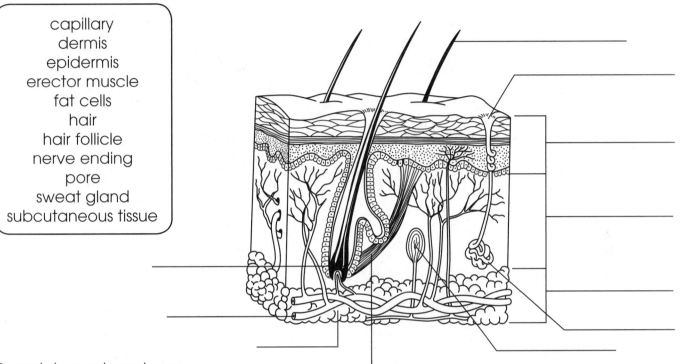

Complete each sentence.

_____ makes up the skin of the body and the lining of the respiratory and digestive tracts. _____ is the largest organ of the vertebrate body, composing 15 percent of the actual weight in an adult. Vertebrate skin is composed of two layers: the outer _____ and the lower _____. The protective underlying layer is called thw _____ layer. Cells are constantly lost from the _____ and replaced by new cells produced deep within the epidermis. It takes about 27 days for all of the outer skin cells to be _____. Specialized cells called melanocytes within the epidermis produce a brownish pigment called _____. People of all races have about the same number of melanocytes but differ in the amount of _____ produced, thus giving a vast range of skin tones. The dermis is composed mainly of _____ tissue, which gives the skin its strength and elasticity. Among the structures in the dermis are blood _____, nerves, hair _____, oil _____, and _____ glands. Wrinkling of the skin occurs in the _____ layer. Leather goods are made of animal _____.

Neuron and Neuromuscular Junction

Label the parts of a neuron.

axon
cell body (cyton)
dendrites
myelin sheath
node of Ranvier
nucleus
Schwann cell
Schwann cell
nucleus
axon terminal
terminal branches

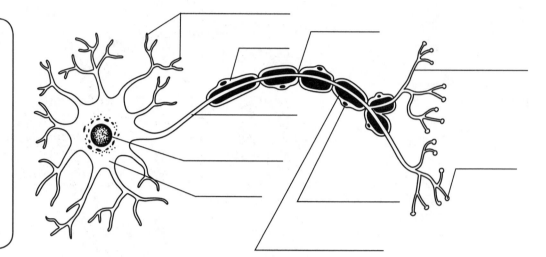

Complete each sentence.

_____ are specialized for the transmission of nerve impulses. The nucleus is located in the _____ of the neuron. From the cell body, two types of structures carry out transmission functions. _____ transmit nerve impulses from other cells or sensory systems. _____ provide for the transmission of nerve impulses away from the cell body. A single neuron cell can be over a meter long due to the length of its _____. _____ are the supporting cells associated with axons. They form a(n) _____ around many vertebrate neurons. _____ interrupt the myelin sheath were the axon is in direct contact with surrounding intercellular fluid. The junction between a neuron and a muscle is called a(n) _____ junction. _____ is the neurotransmitter. At a neuromuscular junction, acetylcholine released from a(n) _____ depolarizes the muscle cell membrane and triggers muscle contractions.

Label the parts of a neuromuscular junction.

axon
cleft
synaptic knob
muscle fiber
acetylcholine sacs

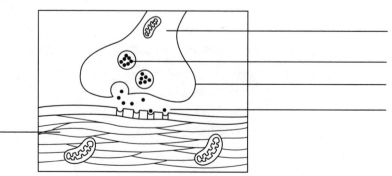

Structure of the Human Eye

Label the parts of the human eye.

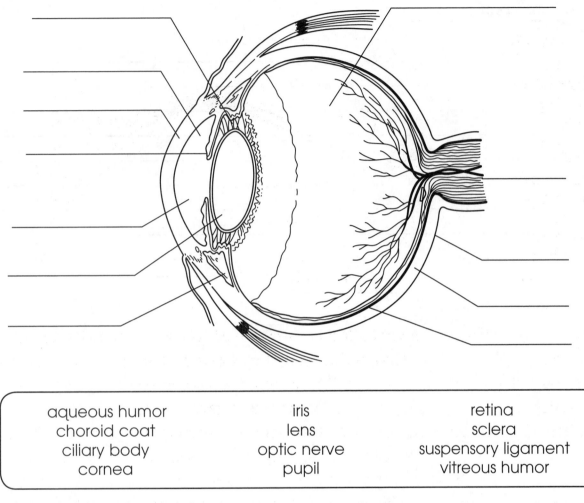

aqueous humor	iris	retina
choroid coat	lens	sclera
ciliary body	optic nerve	suspensory ligament
cornea	pupil	vitreous humor

Complete each sentence.

Light passes through a transparent layer, the _____, which begins to focus the light onto the rear of the eye. Light then passes through the _____, the major focusing structure. The lens is held in place by suspending ligaments to _____. Contraction of these muscles changes the shape of the lens and the _____. The _____, located between the cornea and the lens, controls the amount of light entering the eye. The iris reduces the size of the transparent zone, or _____, of the eye. The _____, in the back of the eye, contains about 3 million _____ that detect color and one billion _____ that detect light and dark. The central region of the retina where images are focused is called the _____. The _____ transmits visual impulses directly to the brain. People whose point of focus lies in front of the fovea are said to be _____. If the point of focus lies behind the fovea, they are called _____. Corrective lenses may be used to focus the image onto the _____, thus correcting the condition.

Structure of the Brain

Label the parts of the brain and spinal cord on the diagram on the left. Give the purpose or function of each part.

cerebellum _____

medulla oblongata _____

thalamus _____

hypothalamus _____

corpus callosum _____

pons _____

spinal cord _____

cerebrum _____

pituitary gland _____

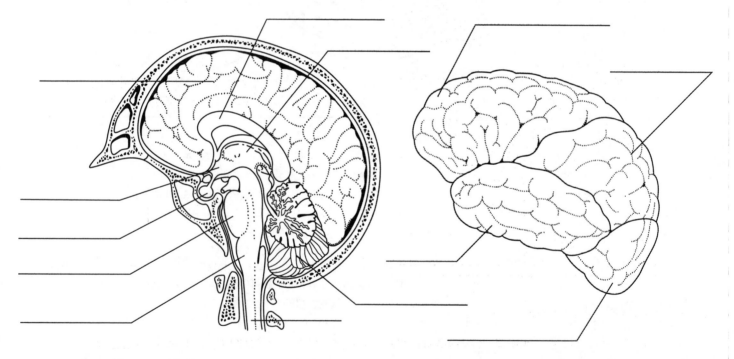

The diagram on the right shows the four major lobes of the cerebrum: frontal, parietal, occipital, and temporal. Label each lobe. Then, complete each sentence.

The _____ lobes control some body movements, reasoning, judgment, and emotions. The sense of vision is located in the _____ lobe. The sense of hearing is interpreted in the _____ lobes. The _____ lobes interpret sensations such as pain, pressure, touch, hot, and cold.

Name_____

Spinal Cord and Reflex Act

Label the parts of a spinal cord on the cross-section diagram.

dorsal root ganglion
gray matter
interneuron
motor neuron
nerve fibers
sensory neuron
synapse
white matter

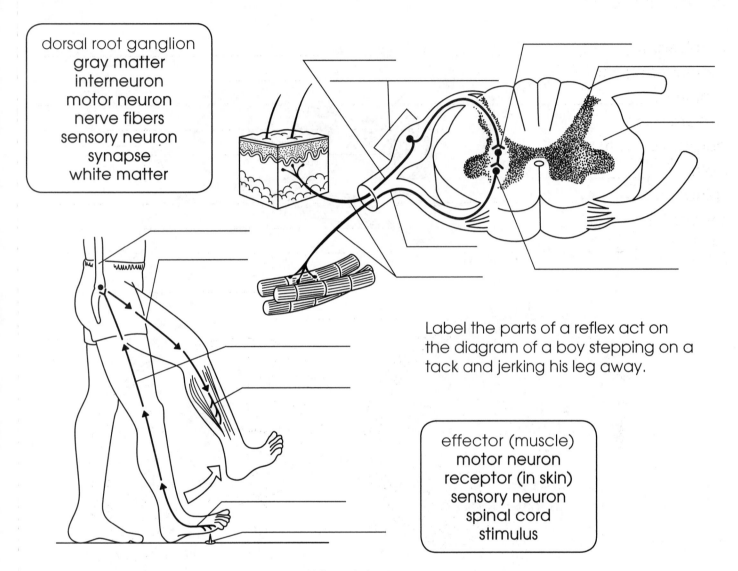

Label the parts of a reflex act on the diagram of a boy stepping on a tack and jerking his leg away.

effector (muscle)
motor neuron
receptor (in skin)
sensory neuron
spinal cord
stimulus

Complete each sentence.

Suppose you stepped on a tack. You jerked your leg away _____ you were aware of what happened. The impulse traveled from the _____, the skin, along a(n) _____ neuron into the _____. The impulse jumped across a(n) _____ to a(an) _____, then across another synapse to a(n) _____ neuron. The impulse traveled along this nerve to a muscle, or _____, in your leg. You jerked your leg away. Only a fraction of a second later, a(n)_____ traveled up your _____ to your _____. But you had _____ reacted. This kind of reaction is known as a(n) _____. Reflex acts occur without thinking.

Structure of the Human Ear

Label the parts of the ear.

anvil
auditory canal
auditory nerve
cochlea
eardrum
earlobe
Eustachian tube
hammer
oval window
semicircular canals
stirrup

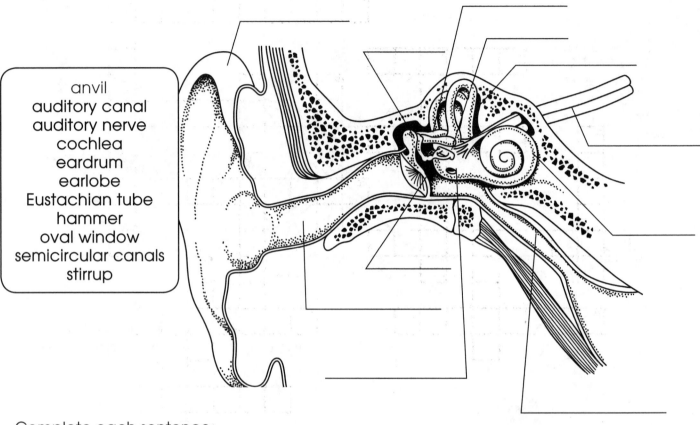

Complete each sentence.

Sound waves beat against a large membrane of the outer ear called the eardrum, or _____. In the _____, these vibrations are transferred by the three small bones, _____, _____, and _____, which increase the force of the vibration. The _____ presses against the _____, which is smaller than the tympanic membrane. The _____ connects the throat to the middle ear and serves to equalize air pressure. Hearing actually takes place on the other side of the oval window, in the _____. The fluid-filled chamber of the inner ear is called the _____. It accepts the wave motion that then travels through the vestibular and tympanic canals. Where the sound waves beat against the sides of the canals, _____ bend and _____ transmit impulses. The _____ carries this information to the brain where it is interpreted. The upper part of the inner ear contains three _____. These are positioned at _____ angles to each other and are filled with _____. The semicircular canals help maintain _____.

Name_____

Nervous System Crossword

Across

1. Inflammation of the membranes around the brain and spinal cord
3. Basic unit of structure and function in the nervous system
7. Controls involuntary activities such as breathing and heartbeat
9. Muscles and glands, for example
10. Largest part of the brain; where thought occurs
11. All nerves that are not part of the central nervous system
14. Complex, unlearned, involuntary behavior
15. Nervous system that controls the voluntary skeletal muscles
16. Damage to the brain due to a hemorrhage or blood clot

Down

2. Nerve pathway between the brain and other parts of the body
4. Sense organs
5. Bundles of neurons that transmit impulses over long distances
6. Part of the brain that coordinates voluntary activities and balance
8. Inborn, involuntary response to a particular stimulus
12. Response repeated constantly until it becomes automatic
13. Nervous system that controls the activities of the internal organs

Structure of the Heart

Label the parts of the human heart.

aorta
bicuspid valve
(mitral valve)
inferior vena cava
left atrium
left pulmonary
artery
left pulmonary vein
left ventricle
right atrium
right pulmonary
artery
right pulmonary
vein
right ventricle
semilunar valves
septum
superior vena cava
tricuspid valve

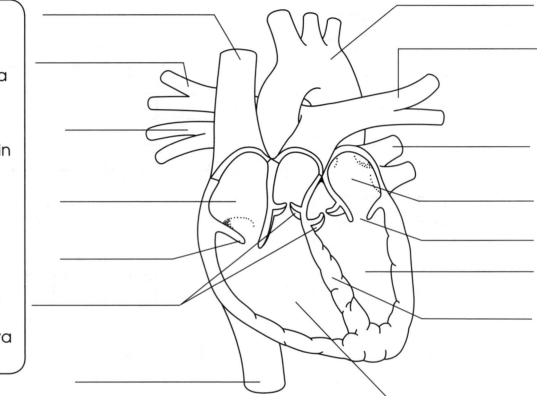

Complete each sentence. Then, label the SA and AV nodes.

The heart beats regularly because it has its own pacemaker. The pacemaker is a small region of muscle called the sinoatrial, or SA, node. It is in the upper back wall of the right _____. The _____ node triggers an impulse that causes both atria to _____. Very quickly, the impulse reaches the atrioventricular, or AV, node at the bottom of the _____ atrium. Immediately, the _____ node triggers an impulse that causes both _____ to contract.

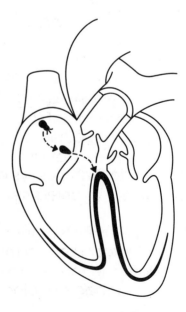

The Human Circulatory System

Starting from and ending with the right atrium, trace the flow of blood through the heart and body by numbering each stage in the correct order.

_____	right atrium	_____	lungs
_____	left atrium	_____	right ventricle
_____	pulmonary artery	_____	left ventricle
_____	vena cava	_____	body cells
_____	aorta	_____	pulmonary veins

Starting from and ending with the heart, trace the flow of blood through the human circulatory system and body by numbering each stage in the correct order.

_____	heart	_____	capillaries
_____	veins	_____	arteries
_____	arterioles	_____	venules

Write the term that best fits each description.

1.   vessels that carry blood away from the heart _____

2.   vessels that carry blood toward the heart _____

3.   tiny blood vessels with walls that are only one cell thick _____

4.   thick wall that divides the heart into two sides _____

5.   upper chambers of the heart that receive blood _____

6.   lower chambers of the heart that pump blood out of the heart _____

7.   valve between right atrium and right ventricle _____

8.   valve between left atrium and left ventricle _____

9.   valves found between the ventricles and blood vessels _____

10.   membrane around the heart _____

11.   the only artery in the body rich in carbon dioxide _____

12.   the only vein in the body rich in oxygen _____

The Blood

Label the parts on the diagram. Then, answer each question.

platelets   red blood cell   white blood cell

1. What is the role of platelets? _____

    _____

    _____

2. What are sickle cells? _____

    _____

    _____

3. Why are they important? _____

    _____

    _____

Match the description with the correct term.

a. iron-containing molecule in red blood cells

b. white blood cells that produce antibodies

c. liquid part of the blood

d. returns tissue fluid to the blood

e. cell fragments involved in clotting

f. foreign molecules in the body

g. cancer of the bone marrow

h. condition in which the blood cannot carry sufficient oxygen

i. strands of protein involved in clotting

j. react with antigens and inactivates them

_____ plasma

_____ platelets

_____ lymphocytes

_____ antigens

_____ fibrin

_____ hemoglobin

_____ antibodies

_____ anemia

_____ leukemia

_____ lymphatic system

Blood Types and Transfusions

Complete the table. Then, answer each question.

Blood Type	Antigens on Red Cells	Antibodies in Plasma	May Donate To	May Receive From
A				
B				
AB				
O				

1. Why are individuals with blood type O considered universal donors? _____
_____

2. Why are individuals with blood type AB considered universal recipients? _____
_____

3. Today, some people who know they must undergo surgery in the near future give their own blood at the blood bank. Then, they use it during surgery. Why?
_____

The distribution of blood types around the world varies. For example, it is different in Japan and among Basque people in northern Spain.

POPULATION	A	B	AB	O
Australia	38%	10%	3%	49%
Philippines	23%	25%	6%	46%
Canada	42%	9%	3%	46%

Blood typing information taken from Australian Red Cross, Red Cross of the Philippines, and Canadian Blood Services

Use the table to answer each question.

1. In Canada, what is the most common blood type? _____

2. If you were Australian, what are the chances that your blood type is A? _____

3. What country has the lowest representation of type A? _____

4. What blood type is least common in all three countries? _____

5. Compare the frequency of type B blood between Australians and Canadians. _____
_____

Name_____

The Human Digestive System

Label the parts of the human digestive system.

anus
appendix
esophagus
gallbladder
large intestine
liver
mouth
pancreas
rectum
salivary glands
small intestine
stomach

Accessory Organs

Food does not pass through three organs in the digestive system. Label these accessory organs in the diagram.

gallbladder
liver
pancreas

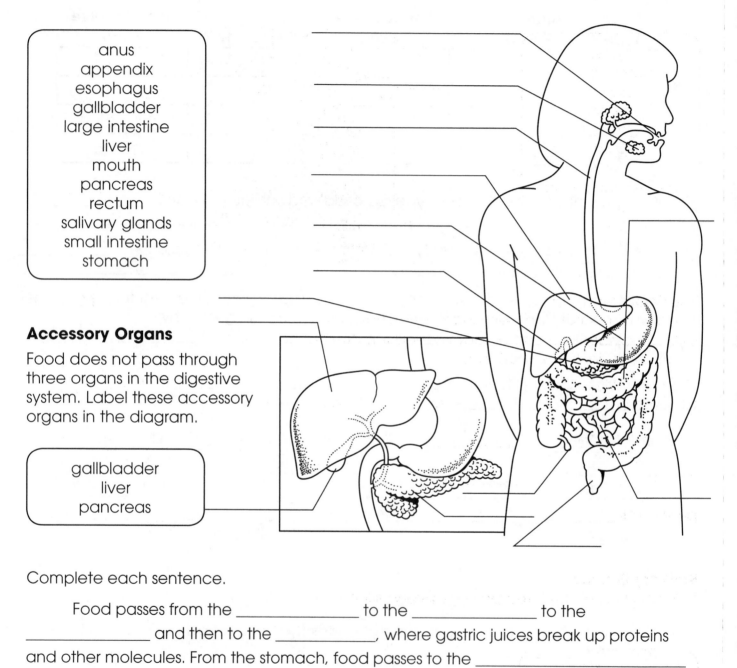

Complete each sentence.

Food passes from the _____ to the _____ to the _____ and then to the _____, where gastric juices break up proteins and other molecules. From the stomach, food passes to the _____ where nutrients are absorbed into the body's bloodstream. Undigested material moves into the _____, or colon, where water is resorbed and the residual material is compacted. This material, now known as feces, moves into the _____ where it is stored temporarily until it passes out of the _____. Above the stomach is the _____, and nested below the stomach is the _____, which secretes many of the digestive enzymes.

84

The Mouth and Teeth

Label the parts of the tooth.

bone
cementum
crown
dentin
enamel
gum
neck
nerves and blood
vessels
pulp
root

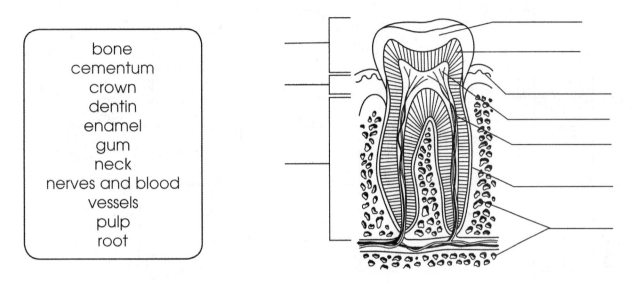

Teeth in Your Jaw

The diagram shows the teeth in the upper jaw. Label the four kinds of teeth. Then, indicate what each kind of tooth is used for: *cutting* food, *tearing and shredding* food, or *grinding and crushing* food.

canines _____

incisors _____

molars _____

premolars _____

Salivary Glands

The mouth contains three pair of salivary glands. Label each gland.

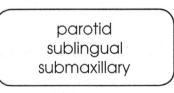

parotid
sublingual
submaxillary

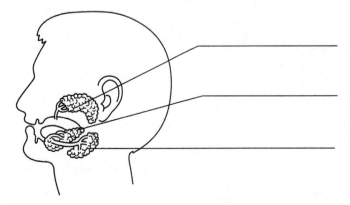

Human Digestive System Crossword

Across

5. Chemical digestion of carbohydrates begins here.
6. Enzyme that begins the digestion of proteins
8. Produced by the liver, this emulsifies fats to make digestion easier.
10. Acid present in the stomach
11. Tube between the mouth and stomach
12. Water and certain vitamins are absorbed here from the undigested food.

Down

1. Wastes are stored here before expulsion.
2. Fingerlike projections that increase the surface area of the small intestine
3. Long, convoluted tube where chemical digestion is completed
4. Enzyme present in saliva
7. Involuntary muscle contraction that moves the food through the digestive system
9. In this muscular pouch, food is mixed with gastric juice.

The Human Respiratory System

Label the parts of the human respiratory system.

alveoli   mouth
bronchi   nasal
bronchiole   passage
diaphragm   nostrils
epiglottis   pharynx
larynx   pleura
lung   trachea

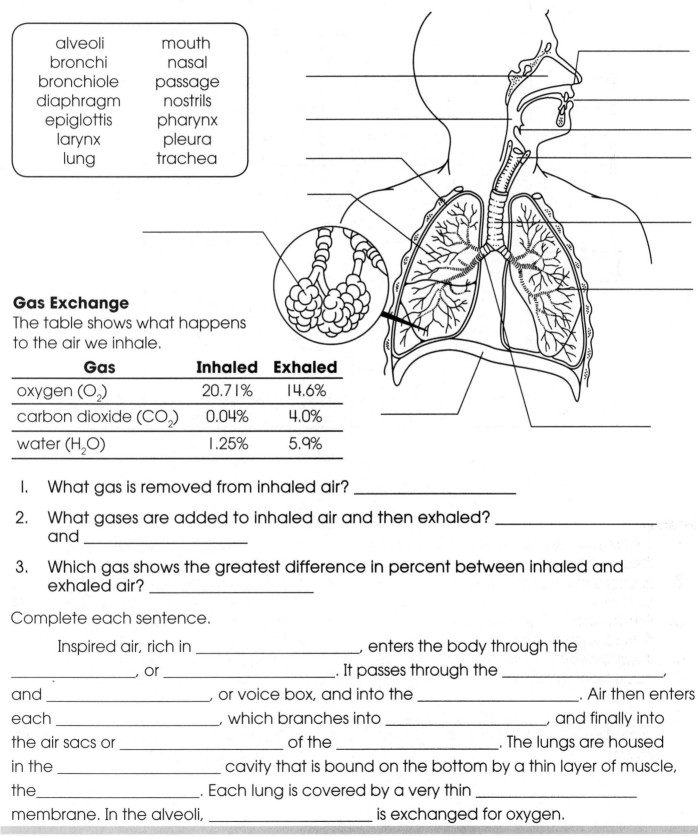

Gas Exchange

The table shows what happens to the air we inhale.

Gas	Inhaled	Exhaled
oxygen (O_2)	20.71%	14.6%
carbon dioxide (CO_2)	0.04%	4.0%
water (H_2O)	1.25%	5.9%

1. What gas is removed from inhaled air? _____

2. What gases are added to inhaled air and then exhaled? _____ and _____

3. Which gas shows the greatest difference in percent between inhaled and exhaled air? _____

Complete each sentence.

Inspired air, rich in _____, enters the body through the _____, or _____. It passes through the _____, and _____, or voice box, and into the _____. Air then enters each _____, which branches into _____, and finally into the air sacs or _____ of the _____. The lungs are housed in the _____ cavity that is bound on the bottom by a thin layer of muscle, the_____. Each lung is covered by a very thin _____ membrane. In the alveoli, _____ is exchanged for oxygen.

Name_____

Human Respiratory System Crossword

Across

3. Area at the back of the throat where the mouth and nasal cavity meet
4. The trachea divides into these right and left branches
5. Opening to the windpipe
7. Contains the vocal cords
10. Tiny air sacs where the exchange of gases between air and blood takes place
11. Flat sheet of muscle separating the chest cavity from the abdominal cavity
14. Inflammation of the lining of the bronchial tubes

Down

1. Smaller branches of the bronchi
2. Flap of tissue that prevents food from entering windpipe during swallowing
6. Tube leading from larynx to bronchi
8. Blood vessels surrounding the air sacs
9. Moist membrane covering the lung and chest cavity wall on each side
12. Infection of the lungs caused by viruses, bacteria, or fungi
13. Bronchial spasm resulting in decreased air movement and air trapped in alveoli

Name_____

The Human Urinary Tract and Kidney

Label the parts of the human urinary system. Give the function or purpose of each part.

kidney _____

adrenal glands _____

ureter _____

urinary bladder _____

_____

urethra _____

_____

renal artery _____

_____

renal vein _____

_____

cortex _____

_____

medulla _____

_____

renal pelvis _____

_____

Complete each sentence.

      Kidneys are the "filters" of the _____ system. They control the essential balance between body salts and _____. They remove from the blood nitrogenous wastes, water, urea, nonvolatile foreign substances, excess salt, and excess water. The kidney is enclosed by a connective tissue _____ and is divided into an outer _____ and an inner _____. The _____ functions chiefly for water resorption. The liquid waste, _____, collected by the kidneys passes through the _____ to the _____. The urinary bladder is a strong muscular organ that stores the urine until it can be excreted via the _____.

The Nephron

Label the parts of a nephron.

Bowman's capsule
capillaries
collecting tubule
glomerulus
loop of Henle
renal arteriole

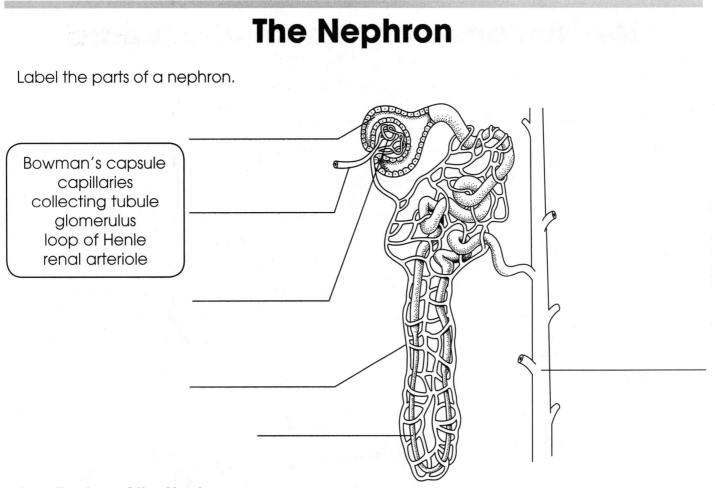

Functioning of the Nephron

The diagram indicates that the nephrons remove wastes from the blood by the process of filtration and reabsorption. Filtration takes place in the glomerulus; reabsorption takes place in the loop of Henle.

Label the areas where filtration and reabsorption take place. Tell whether each of the following substances that is filtered from the blood in the glomerulus is reabsorbed, excreted as part of the urine, or both.

water_____

amino acids _____

glucose_____

salt _____

urea _____

Human Excretory System Crossword

Across

2. Tubes connecting the kidneys to the urinary bladder
3. Carbon dioxide and water are excreted here during exhalation
6. Structures in the skin that excrete water, salts, and some urea
8. Urine is expelled from the body through this tube
10. Arteries and veins to kidneys

Down

1. Microscopic units that filter the blood in the kidneys
2. Liquid waste collected and excreted by the kidneys
3. Removes toxic substances from the blood and converts excess amino acids to urea
4. Organs that filter wastes and other dissolved substances out of the blood
5. The urinary ____ stores the urine until it can be excreted by the body.
7. Endocrine gland at the top of each kidney
9. Loop of ____ at the bottom of nephron

Name_____

The Human Endocrine System

Label the parts of the human endocrine system.

adrenal
hypothalamus
ovary (female)
pancreas
parathyroids
pineal
pituitary
testis (male)
thymus
thyroid

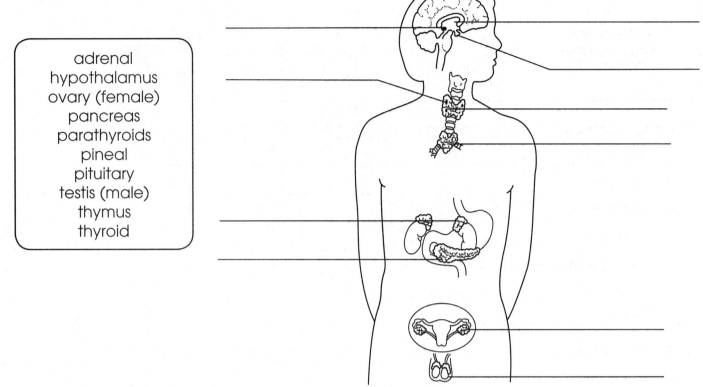

Complete each sentence.

1. The _____ gland may control biorhythms in some animals and controls the onset of puberty in humans.

2. The _____ gland stimulates metabolic rate and is essential to normal growth and development.

3. The _____ gland stimulates growth and stimulates secretion of hormones from other glands.

4. The _____ gland promotes production and maturation of white blood cells.

5. The _____ is the major area where the nervous and endocrine systems interact.

6. The _____ controls blood glucose levels and determines the fate of glycogen.

7. The _____ gland initiates stress responses, increases heart rate, blood pressure, and metabolic rate, dilates blood vessels, mobilizes fat, and raises blood sugar levels.

8. _____ in females stimulate development of secondary sex characteristics, stimulate growth of sex organs at puberty, and prompt monthly preparation of uterus for pregnancy.

9. _____ in males stimulate development of secondary sex characteristics, stimulate a growth spurt at puberty, and stimulate spermatogenesis.

10. The _____ gland increases blood calcium level, stimulates calcium reabsorption, and activates vitamin D.

Human Hormones

The major hormones produced by the human body are:

ACTH	cortisol	insulin	prolactin
adrenaline	estrogen	Luteinizing hormone	testosterone
aldosterone	FSH	noradrenaline	thyroxin
calcitonin	glucagon	parathormone	TSH
	growth hormone	progesterone	

Next to each gland, write the name of the hormone or hormones it produces.

1. pituitary _____

2. thyroid _____

3. parathyroid _____

4. adrenal _____

5. pancreas (islets of Langerhans)_____

6. testis _____

7. ovary _____

Next to each function, write the name of the hormone that produces this effect.

8. raises the blood sugar level and increases the heartbeat and breathing rates _____

9. causes glucose to be removed from the blood and stored _____

10. influences the development of female secondary sex characteristics _____

11. promotes the conversion of glycogen to glucose _____

12. controls the metabolism of calcium _____

13. promotes the reabsorbation of sodium and potassium ions by the kidney _____

14. influences the development of male secondary sex characteristics _____

15. stimulates the elongation of the long bones of the body _____

16. stimulates the secretion of hormones by the cortex of the adrenal glands _____

17. regulates the rate of metabolism in the body _____

18. stimulates the development of eggs in the female's ovary _____

19. involved in the regulation of carbohydrate, protein, and fat metabolism _____

20. stimulates the production of thyroxin _____

Name_____

Structure of a Bird's Egg

Label the parts of the newly fertilized bird's egg and the developing bird's egg in the diagrams. Give the function or purpose of each part.

shell _____

amnion _____

amniotic fluid _____

embryo _____

chorion _____

yolk sac _____

blood vessels _____

allantois _____

albumin _____

air space _____

shell membrane _____

yolk _____

chalaza _____

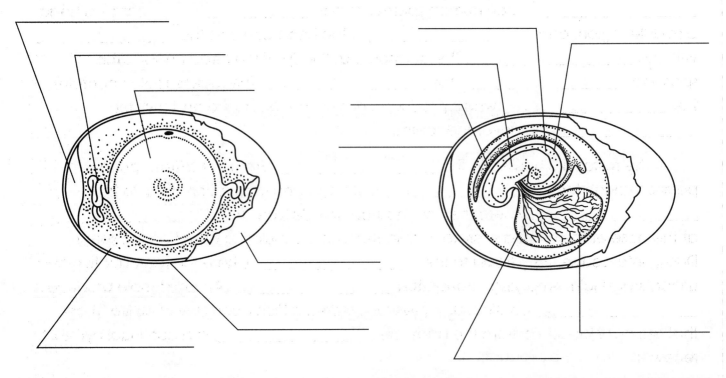

Name_____

The Male Reproductive System

Label the parts of the male reproductive system.

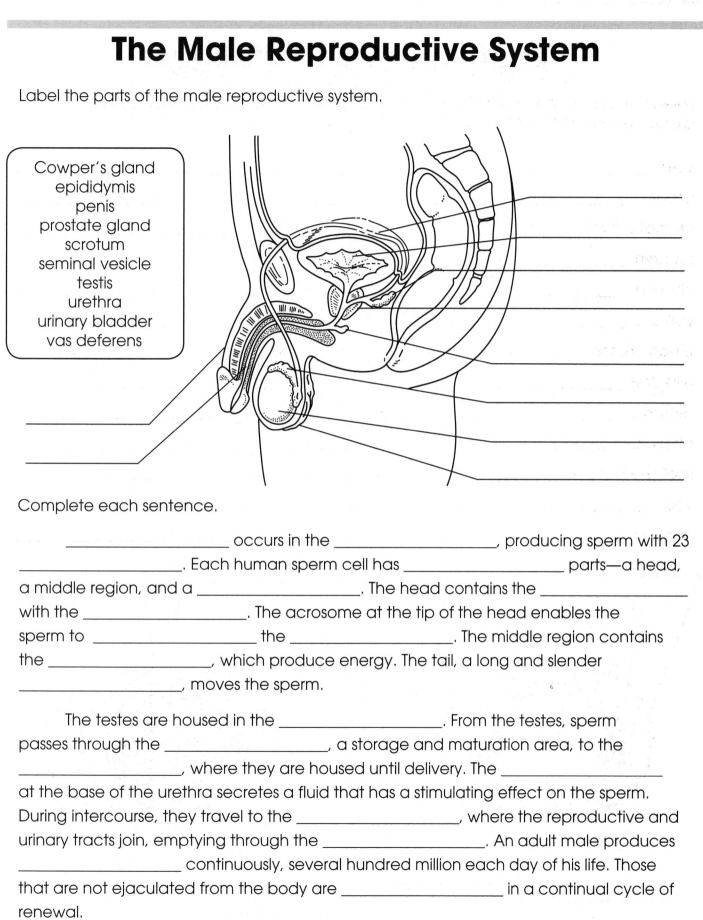

Cowper's gland
epididymis
penis
prostate gland
scrotum
seminal vesicle
testis
urethra
urinary bladder
vas deferens

Complete each sentence.

_____ occurs in the _____, producing sperm with 23 _____. Each human sperm cell has _____ parts—a head, a middle region, and a _____. The head contains the _____ with the _____. The acrosome at the tip of the head enables the sperm to _____ the _____. The middle region contains the _____, which produce energy. The tail, a long and slender _____, moves the sperm.

The testes are housed in the _____. From the testes, sperm passes through the _____, a storage and maturation area, to the _____, where they are housed until delivery. The _____ at the base of the urethra secretes a fluid that has a stimulating effect on the sperm. During intercourse, they travel to the _____, where the reproductive and urinary tracts join, emptying through the _____. An adult male produces _____ continuously, several hundred million each day of his life. Those that are not ejaculated from the body are _____ in a continual cycle of renewal.

The Female Reproductive System

Label the parts of the female reproductive system.

cervix
Fallopian tube
ovary
urethra
urinary bladder
uterus
vagina

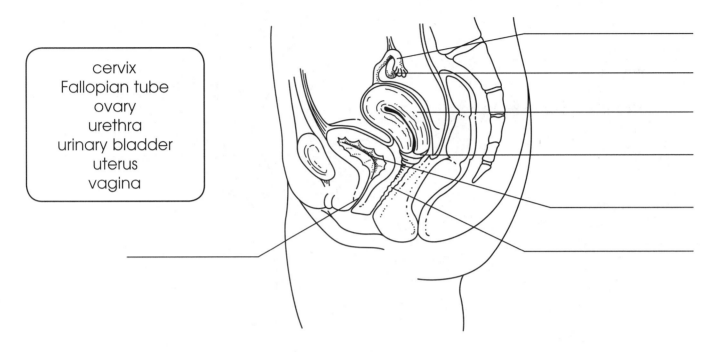

Complete each sentence.

The female is born with about two million _____ halted at prophase I, only 400 of which will mature into _____ within her lifetime. On about the _____ day of the menstrual cycle, the ovum is released from a _____ on the surface of the _____ at ovulation. _____ move it into the _____. Sperm are deposited in the _____, which leads to the mouth of the _____. They must make their way through the _____ (the muscular sphincter at the opening of the uterus), through the uterus, and up the Fallopian tube to fertilize the ovum within about 24 hours or the ovum will die. Peristaltic contractions move the ovum or zygote to the _____ in about three days. If the ovum is not fertilized and implanted, _____ will occur on day 28.

In any egg cell, the sex chromosome is a(n) _____ chromosome. In a sperm cell, the sex chromosome is either a(n) _____ or a(n) _____ chromosome. If a sperm with an X chromosome fertilized the egg, the sex chromosome pattern of the fertilized egg is _____, and the offspring will be a _____. If a sperm with a Y chromosome fertilizes the egg, the sex chromosome pattern of the fertilized egg is _____, and the offspring will be a _____.

A Mammal Embryo

Label the parts of the embryo in utero. Give the function or purpose of each part.

embryo _____

placenta _____

Fallopian tube _____

uterine wall _____

umbilical cord _____

_____

_____

amnion _____

_____

_____

amniotic fluid _____

_____

_____

vagina _____

_____

_____

uterus _____

_____

_____

Complete each sentence.

After two months of development, the embryo is called a(n) _____.
The _____ is formed in part from the inner lining of the uterus and in part
from other membranes. It is through the placenta that the embryo/fetus is nourished
while in the _____ and _____ are carried away. The
_____ connects the embryo/fetus with the placenta. It provides a transport
system for placental-fetal circulation. The _____ is the innermost of the
extra embryonic membranes, and it forms a fluid-filled _____ around the
embryo or fetus.

Human Reproduction

Complete each sentence using the word list. Words may be used more than once.

The production of sperm takes place in the _____. These paired glands are contained in a sac called the _____. The sperm travel to the urethra through a long tube called the _____. During this passage, _____, secreted by the _____, _____, and Cowper's glands, are mixed with the sperm. This mixture is called _____. During sexual intercourse, _____ is released through the urethra and deposited in the female's _____. The female gonad is called the _____. A female is born with all of the egg cells, or _____, that she will ever have, but they are immature. Beginning at _____, the hormone _____ is released from the pituitary to stimulate maturation of eggs. The eggs are contained in saclike structures called _____. Usually, only one of the eggs matures fully each month. As the _____ enlarge, they secrete the hormone _____, which causes the lining of the _____ to thicken. After about 9 to 19 days, a surge of the hormone _____ is released from the pituitary gland. This causes the fully developed _____ to rupture, releasing a mature egg. This is called _____. The empty follicle now becomes a mass of yellow tissue called the _____. This secretes the hormone _____ which further thickens the lining of the uterus in preparation for receiving and nourishing a fertilized egg. When the ovum is released during _____, it enters a _____ and begins its journey to the uterus. If it encounters sperm during this journey, it may be fertilized and begin dividing. When the fertilized egg reaches the uterus, if all goes well, _____ will occur and a pregnancy will be established. If no fertilization occurs, the _____ disintegrates in 13–15 days and _____ occurs. Then the cycle begins again.

corpus luteum	implantation	ovulation	seminal fluid
estrogen	LH (luteinizing hormone)	progesterone	seminal vesicles
Fallopian tube	menstruation	prostate	testes
follicles	ova	puberty	uterus
FSH (follicle stimulating hormone)	ovary	scrotum	vagina
		semen	vas deferens

Human Endocrine and Reproduction Crossword

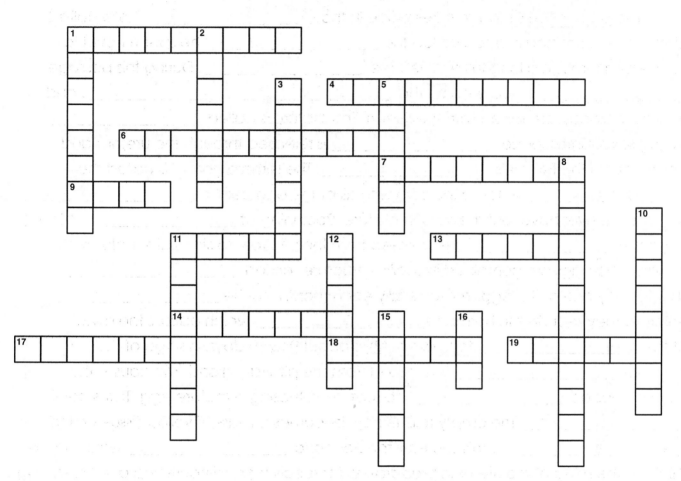

Across

1. Endocrine gland at base of brain
4. Hormone that causes follicle to mature
6. At the base of brain, gland that interacts with pituitary
7. Hormone produced by thyroid
9. Pituitary hormone that targets adrenal
11. Organ through which sperm leaves the body
13. Tube leading from uterus to outside of body
14. Sac containing testes
18. Houses developing embryo
19. Fluid-filled membrane surrounding embryo

Down

1. Gland that secretes insulin
2. Gland that secretes thyroxin
3. Organs that produce egg cells
5. Male reproductive glands
8. Hormone produced by adrenal medulla
10. Uterine membrane; transports substances between mother and embryo
11. A gland that secretes seminal fluid
17. Tube joining ovary to uterus
12. Ductless gland under breastbone
15. Neck of uterus
16. Hormone stimulates follicle production

Types of Diseases

Diseases may be classified into several types; among these are inherited diseases, deficiency diseases, infectious diseases, and hormonal diseases.

First, identify the type of disease as *deficiency*, *infectious*, or *hormonal*. Then, identify the specific cause of each disease. For inherited diseases, indicate whether it is sex-linked or the result of a defective gene or chromosome.

Disease	Type of Disease	Specific Cause
1. tetanus	_____	_____
2. diabetes	_____	_____
3. hemophilia	_____	_____
4. common cold	_____	_____
5. sickle-cell anemia	_____	_____
6. measles	_____	_____
7. Addison's disease	_____	_____
8. anemia	_____	_____
9. Down syndrome	_____	_____
10. AIDS	_____	_____
11. night blindness	_____	_____
12. tuberculosis	_____	_____
13. polio	_____	_____
14. Kleinfelter syndrome	_____	_____
15. colorblindness	_____	_____
16. pellagra	_____	_____
17. goiter	_____	_____
18. diptheria	_____	_____
19. rickets	_____	_____
20. pertussis	_____	_____

Metamorphosis

As insects develop, they undergo **metamorphosis**, a series of definite changes in appearance. Some insects, such as a butterfly, undergo complete metamorphosis. Other insects, such as the grasshopper, undergo incomplete metamorphosis.

Label the stages on the diagram of the complete metamorphosis of the butterfly and incomplete metamorphosis of the grasshopper.

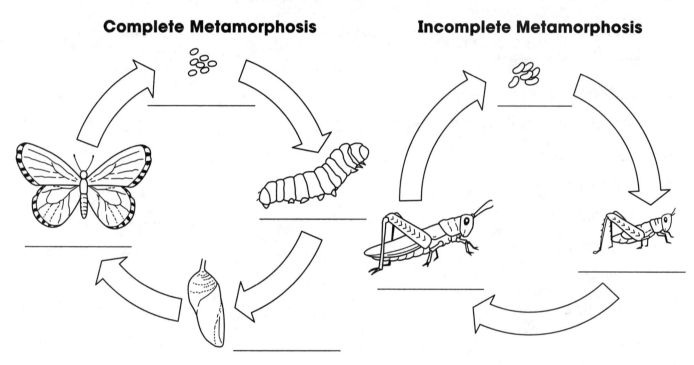

Complete each sentence.

In complete metamorphosis, a female butterfly hatches into a wormlike organism called a _____, or caterpillar. During this stage, the organism consumes a large amount of food. The _____, or caterpillar, then spins a protective covering around itself and becomes a(n) _____, or chrysalis. This covering is called a _____. While inside this covering, the _____ changes into a(n) _____.

In _____ metamorphosis, a grasshopper goes through a(n) _____ change from egg to _____. The grasshopper begins as a(n) _____ and hatches into a(n) _____. A nymph is an immature _____ that resembles a full-grown grasshopper but lacks _____. As the nymph grows, it _____ until it reaches the last stage, the _____.

Evolution

Five evidences of evolution are fossil evidence (*a*), homologous structures (*b*), embryology (*c*), vestigial organs (*d*), and biochemical (*e*). Write the letter of the type of evidence by each example.

_____ 1. Bones in a bird's wing and a human's arm are similar in structure.

_____ 2. All organisms use ATP in energy transfers.

_____ 3. There are similarities in structure amog the early stages of fish, birds, and humans.

_____ 4. Humans, unlike rabbits, have no known use for their appendix.

_____ 5. Horses have increased in size and decreased in number of toes since the Eocene.

Match the terms with the correct definition or name.

_____ 1. genetic drift

_____ 2. gradualism

_____ 3. natural selection

_____ 4. divergent evolution

_____ 5. punctuated equilibrium

_____ 6. mass extinction

_____ 7. mutations

_____ 8. gene pool

_____ 9. convergent evolution

_____ 10. radioactive dating

_____ 11. use and disuse

a. all genes in a population

b. brief periods of change interrupt long stable periods

c. changes in gene frequency in small populations

d. changes occur gradually over time

e. Darwin

f. determing age of fossils

g. gene or chromosomal changes

h. Lamarck

i. many species vanish at one time

j. unrelated species become less alike

k. unrelated species become more alike

Number the steps of Darwin's Theory of Evolution in order.

_____ Struggle for Existence   _____ Natural Selection

_____ Overproduction   _____ Variation

Answer Key

Name_____

Laboratory Equipment

Label the pieces of laboratory equipment.

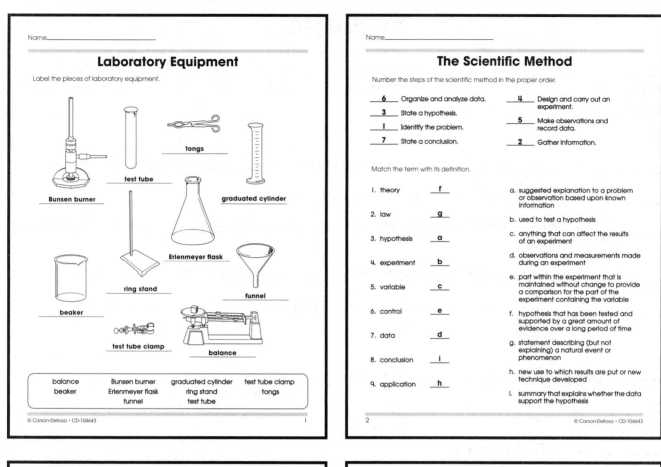

Bunsen burner

test tube

tongs

graduated cylinder

Erlenmeyer flask

ring stand

funnel

beaker

test tube clamp

balance

balance	Bunsen burner	graduated cylinder	test tube clamp
beaker	Erlenmeyer flask	ring stand	tongs
	funnel	test tube	

Name_____

The Scientific Method

Number the steps of the scientific method in the proper order.

__6__ Organize and analyze data.

__3__ State a hypothesis.

__1__ Identify the problem.

__7__ State a conclusion.

__4__ Design and carry out an experiment.

__5__ Make observations and record data.

__2__ Gather information.

Match the term with its definition.

1. theory ____f____

2. law ____g____

3. hypothesis ____a____

4. experiment ____b____

5. variable ____c____

6. control ____e____

7. data ____d____

8. conclusion ____i____

9. application ____h____

a. suggested explanation to a problem or observation based upon known information

b. used to test a hypothesis

c. anything that can affect the results of an experiment

d. observations and measurements made during an experiment

e. part within the experiment that is maintained without change to provide a comparison for the part of the experiment containing the variable

f. hypothesis that has been tested and supported by a great amount of evidence over a long period of time

g. statement describing (but not explaining) a natural event or phenomenon

h. new use to which results are put or new technique developed

i. summary that explains whether the data support the hypothesis

---

Name_____

The Systeme International D'Unites (SI)

The measuring system used in science is the SI, which was adopted according to an international agreement reached in 1960. It is based on the metric system. The standard units in SI are:

Property	Unit	Symbol
mass	kilogram	kg
distance	meter	m
time	second	s
electric current	ampere	A
temperature	Kelvin	K
amount of substance	mole	mol

As with the metric system, the SI utilizes prefixes to change the value of units. The units frequently used in science are:

Prefix	Symbol	Value
mega-	M	1 000 000
kilo-	k	1 000
deci-	d	0.1
centi-	c	0.01
milli-	m	0.001
micro-	μ	0.000 001
nano-	n	0.000 000 0001

Example
How many meters are equivalent to 500 mm?

$500 \text{ mm} \times \dfrac{1 \text{ m}}{1{,}000 \text{ mm}} = 0.5 \text{ m}$

Make each conversion within the SI.

1. 3.0 m = __300__ cm

2. 1,500 mL = __1.5__ L

3. 35 cg = __0.35__ g

4. 0.05 m = __50__ mm

5. 2.5 L = __2500__ mL

6. 0.25 km = __250__ m

7. 50,000 μm = __0.05__ m

8. 0.015 g = __15__ mg

9. 75 cL = __0.75__ L

10. 2,750 mg = __2.75__ g

What would a reasonable unit use to measure each measurement?

11. distance from earth to moon _____kilometers_____

12. length of a bacterium _____nanometers_____

13. mass of a bowling ball _____kilogram_____

14. mass of an aspirin tablet _____milligram_____

15. dropperful of medicine _____milliliter_____

Name_____

Self Quiz: Scientific Method and the SI System

Circle the letter of the correct answer.

1. In an experiment, one _____ is tested at a time to determine how it affects results.
   a. control   **b. variable**   c. problem   d. observation

2. The _____ describes the use of equipment and materials in an experiment.
   a. procedure   b. conclusion   c. control   d. problem

3. A _____ is the part of an experiment that provides a reliable standard for comparison.
   a. procedure   b. theory   c. variable   **d. control**

4. The information already recorded about a scientific subject is the scientific _____.
   a. record   b. method   c. technique   d. experiment

5. _____ are the recorded facts and measurements from an experiment.
   a. Procedures   **b. Data**   c. Theories   d. Inferences

6. The practical use of scientific knowledge is called _____.
   a. research   b. inferring   c. procedure   **d. technology**

7. A _____ is an explanation of observations that have been tested many times.
   a. conclusion   b. hypothesis   **c. theory**   d. record

8. A(n) _____ is a suggested solution to a scientific problem.
   a. observation   **b. hypothesis**   c. problem   d. procedure

9. Instruments and our senses are used to make _____ during an experiment.
   a. observations   b. hypotheses   c. problems   d. controls

10. A(n) _____ is performed under carefully controlled conditions to test a hypothesis.
    a. activity   b. observation   **c. inference**   d. experiment

11. A scientific _____ describes how nature works.
    a. record   **b. law**   c. hypothesis   d. result

12. To be accepted, a scientific discovery must produce _____ each time it is tested.
    a. the same results   b. the same hypothesis   c. new conclusions   d. new data

13. If after numerous tests a major hypothesis cannot be shown to be false, it may be accepted as _____.
    a. a control   **b. a theory**   c. data   d. an observation

14. New observations that do not agree with an accepted theory may cause the theory to be _____.
    a. explained   **b. rejected**   c. proven   d. recognized

---

Answer Key

Self Quiz (Continued)

Name_____

15. A _____ is a logical explanation to a problem based on observation.
    a. control   b. theory   c. conclusion   d. procedure
16. A temperature scale having an abosolute zero below which temperatures do not exist.
    a. Kelvin   b. Celsius   c. Fahrenheit   d. the boiling point
17. The _____ is the unit of time in the SI system.
    a. day   b. second   c. minute   d. hour
18. A _____ is a fixed quantity used for comparison.
    a. procedure   b. variable   c. standard   d. prefix
19. The unit of mass commonly used in the laboratory is the _____.
    a. meter   b. cubic meter   c. gram   d. kilometer
20. The space occupied by an object is its _____.
    a. volume   b. height   c. width   d. length
21. The amount of matter in an object is its _____.
    a. mass   b. volume   c. size   d. balance
22. A scale commonly used by scientists for measuring temperature is the _____ scale.
    a. degree   b. Celsius   c. boiling point   d. Fahrenheit
23. One kilogram has _____.
    a. 0.001 grams   b. 1,000 milligrams   c. 0.001 milligrams   d. 1,000 grams
24. Standards are important for comparing observations and are used _____.
    a. by everyone   c. only for counting things
    b. only in tropical rain forests   d. only in scientific experiments
25. One-hundredth of a meter is written as a _____.
    a. decimeter   b. millimeter   c. centimeter   d. kilometer
26. How many millimeters make a centimeter?
    a. 100   b. 10   c. 1,000   d. 0.10
27. A prefix meaning one thousand standard units is _____.
    a. milli-   b. centi-   c. kilo-   d. deci-
28. On the Celsius scale, water boils at what temperature?
    a. 32 degrees   b. 212 degrees   c. 0 degrees   d. 100 degrees
29. Which quantity would equal 50 cc of water?
    a. 5,000 mL   b. 500 mL   c. 50 mL   d. 0.5 L
30. Which of the following units would we use to measure the distance to Australia?
    a. millimeters   b. centimeters   c. kilometers   d. kilograms

---

The Compound Microscope

Name_____

Label each part on the compound microscope. Describe the purpose or use of each part.

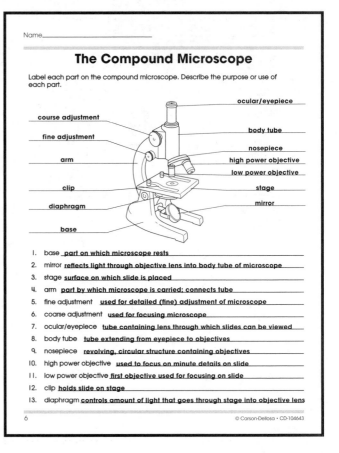

ocular/eyepiece
body tube
nosepiece
high power objective
low power objective
stage
mirror
course adjustment
fine adjustment
arm
clip
diaphragm
base

1. base __part on which microscope rests__
2. mirror __reflects light through objective lens into body tube of microscope__
3. stage __surface on which slide is placed__
4. arm __part by which microscope is carried; connects tube__
5. fine adjustment __used for detailed (fine) adjustment of microscope__
6. coarse adjustment __used for focusing microscope__
7. ocular/eyepiece __tube containing lens through which slides can be viewed__
8. body tube __tube extending from eyepiece to objectives__
9. nosepiece __revolving, circular structure containing objectives__
10. high power objective __used to focus on minute details on slide__
11. low power objective __first objective used for focusing on slide__
12. clip __holds slide on stage__
13. diaphragm __controls amount of light that goes through stage into objective lens__

Microscope Crossword

Name_____

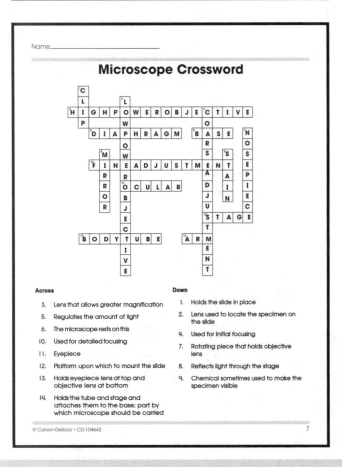

Across

3. Lens that allows greater magnification
5. Regulates the amount of light
6. The microscope rests on this
10. Used for detailed focusing
11. Eyepiece
12. Platform upon which to mount the slide
13. Holds eyepiece lens at top and objective lens at bottom
14. Holds the tube and stage and attaches them to the base; part by which microscope should be carried

Down

1. Holds the slide in place
2. Lens used to locate the specimen on the slide
4. Used for initial focusing
7. Rotating piece that holds objective lens
8. Reflects light through the stage
9. Chemical sometimes used to make the specimen visible

States of Matter

Name_____

Complete the table by placing a check mark in each column that applies. Then, identify its state as *solid*, *liquid*, or *gas*.

Example	Definite Shape	Definite Volume	Takes Shape of Container	State of Matter
water at 25°C		✓	✓	liquid
ice at -4°C	✓	✓		solid
steam at 105°C			✓	gas
iron	✓	✓		solid
air			✓	gas
carbon dioxide at 20°C			✓	gas
juice		✓	✓	liquid
wood	✓	✓		solid
oil		✓	✓	liquid
nitrogen at room temprature			✓	gas
milk		✓	✓	liquid
ozone			✓	gas
glass	✓	✓		solid
coffee		✓	✓	liquid
chalk	✓	✓		solid

Answer Key

Chemical vs. Physical Change

In a **physical change**, the original substance still exists; it has only changed in form. Energy changes usually only accompany physical changes in phase changes and when substances dissolve. In a **chemical change**, a new substance is produced. Energy changes always accompany chemical changes. Physical changes usually accompany chemical changes.

Classify each situation as a *chemical* or a *physical* change.

1. Sodium chloride dissolves in water. __physical__
2. Hydrochloric acid reacts with sodium hydroxide to produce a salt, water, and heat. __chemical__
3. A pellet of sodium is sliced in half. __physical__
4. Water is heated and changes to steam. __physical__
5. Food is digested. __chemical__
6. Starch molecules are formed from smaller glucose molecules. __chemical__
7. Ice melts. __physical__
8. Plant leaves lose water through evaporation. __physical__
9. A red blood cell placed in distilled water swells and bursts. __physical__
10. The energy in food molecules is transferred into molecules of ATP. __chemical__
11. The roots of a plant absorb water. __physical__
12. Iron rusts. __chemical__
13. Oxygen is incorporated into hemoglobin to bring it to the cells. __chemical__
14. A person gets cooler by perspiring. __physical__
15. Proteins are made from amino acids. __chemical__
16. A match burns. __chemical__
17. A toothpick is broken in half. __physical__

Elements, Compounds, and Mixtures

An **element** consists of only one kind of atom. A **compound** consists of two or more different elements chemically combined in a fixed ratio. A **mixture** can have components in any proportion, and those components are not chemically bound.

Classify each item as an element (*E*), compound (*C*), or mixture (*M*).

1. sodium — E
2. water — C
3. soil — M
4. coffee — M
5. oxygen — E
6. alcohol — C
7. carbon dioxide — C
8. cake batter — M
9. air — M
10. soap — M
11. iron — E
12. salt water — M
13. ice cream — M
14. nitrogen — E
15. eggs — M
16. blood — M
17. table salt — C
18. nail polish — M
19. milk — M
20. cola — M

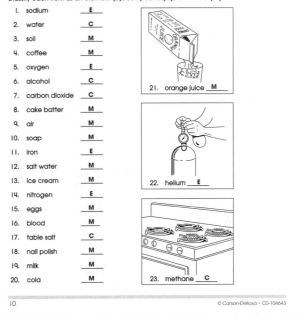

21. orange juice — M

22. helium — E

23. methane — C

Element Symbols

These elements are common in living organisms. Write the symbol for each one.

1. oxygen — O
2. hydrogen — H
3. chlorine — Cl
4. potassium — K
5. fluorine — F
6. manganese — Mn
7. carbon — C
8. zinc — Zn
9. sodium — Na
10. sulfur — S
11. phosphorus — P
12. iodine — I
13. magnesium — Mg
14. nitrogen — N
15. copper — Cu
16. iron — Fe
17. calcium — Ca
18. cobalt — Co

Write the name of the element indicated by each symbol.

19. As — arsenic
20. Pb — lead
21. Kr — krypton
22. Ba — barium
23. He — helium
24. Ne — neon
25. Si — silicon
26. U — uranium
27. Sn — tin
28. Pt — platinum
29. Rn — radon
30. Al — aluminum
31. Cu — copper
32. Ag — silver
33. Pu — plutonium
34. Sr — strontium
35. Am — americium
36. Au — gold
37. Ra — radium
38. Ge — germanium
39. Br — bromine
40. Hg — mercury

Parts of the Atom

Using the information provided, determine the number of protons, neutrons, and electrons in each atom. Draw a model of the atom showing the electrons in the proper energy levels.

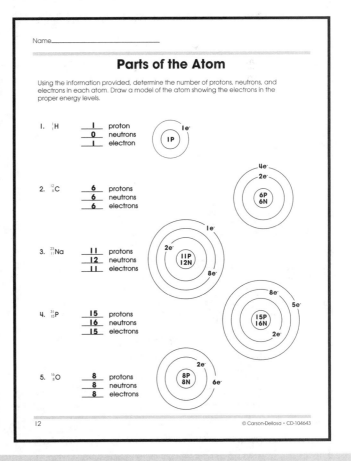

1. $_1^1 H$ — 1 proton, 0 neutrons, 1 electron

2. $_6^{12} C$ — 6 protons, 6 neutrons, 6 electrons

3. $_{11}^{23} Na$ — 11 protons, 12 neutrons, 11 electrons

4. $_{15}^{31} P$ — 15 protons, 16 neutrons, 15 electrons

5. $_8^{16} O$ — 8 protons, 8 neutrons, 8 electrons

Answer Key

Ionic vs. Covalent Bonds

Nonmetals chemically bond by sharing electrons. The bond is called a **covalent bond**. When an active metal and a nonmetal bond, the active metal transfers one or more electrons to the nonmetal. This bond is called an **ionic bond**. Ionic compounds (except for bases) are also called **salts**.

Classify each compound as *ionic* or *covalent*.

1. $CaCl_2$ — **ionic**
2. CO_2 — **covalent**
3. H_2O — **covalent**
4. $BaCl_2$ — **ionic**
5. O_2 — **covalent**
6. NaF — **ionic**
7. NaS — **ionic**
8. S_8 — **covalent**
9. SO_3 — **covalent**
10. $LiBr$ — **ionic**
11. MgO — **ionic**
12. C_2H_5OH — **covalent**
13. HCl — **covalent**
14. N_2 — **covalent**
15. NaI — **ionic**
16. NO_2 — **covalent**
17. Al_2O_3 — **ionic**
18. $FeCl_3$ — **ionic**
19. P_2O_5 — **covalent**
20. N_2O_3 — **covalent**
21. H_2 — **covalent**
22. K_2O — **ionic**
23. KI — **ionic**
24. P_4 — **covalent**
25. CH_4 — **covalent**
26. $NaCl$ — **ionic**

Draw an electron shell diagram of the ionic compound calcium oxide, CaO.

Draw an electron shell diagram of the covalent compound methane, CH_4.

13

Balancing Equations

Balance each chemical equation.

1. $2Na + I_2 \longrightarrow 2NaI$
2. $2N_2 + O_2 \longrightarrow 2N_2O$
3. $N_2 + 3H_2 \longrightarrow 2NH_3$
4. $CH_4 + 2O_2 \longrightarrow CO_2 + 2H_2O$
5. $2KI + Cl_2 \longrightarrow 2KCl + I_2$
6. $2S + 3O_2 \longrightarrow 2SO_3$
7. $2H_2O_2 \longrightarrow 2H_2O + O_2$
8. $2Na + 2H_2O \longrightarrow 2NaOH + H_2$
9. $2H_2O \longrightarrow 2H_2 + O_2$
10. $2KClO_3 \longrightarrow 2KCl + 3O_2$
11. $K_3PO_4 + 3HCl \longrightarrow 3KCl + H_3PO_4$
12. $CO_2 + H_2O \longrightarrow H_2CO_3$ **Already balanced.**
13. $K_2O + H_2O \longrightarrow 2KOH$
14. $Mg + 2HCl \longrightarrow MgCl_2 + H_2$
15. $2KOH + H_2SO_4 \longrightarrow K_2SO_4 + 2H_2O$

14

Self Quiz: Atomic Structure and Equations

Circle the letter of the correct answer.

1. A(n) _____ is a substance made up of one kind of atom.
   a. compound   b. **element**   c. mixture   d. enzyme
2. The smallest particle of an element having the properties of that element is a(n) _____.
   a. **atom**   b. compound   c. molecule   d. enzyme
3. A(n) _____ is matter made of substances that are not chemically bonded together.
   a. **mixture**   b. element   c. compound   d. molecule
4. The correctly written symbol for chlorine is _____.
   a. C   b. CL   c. Ch   d. **Cl**
5. How many atoms of hydrogen are in each molecule of table sugar, $C_{12}H_{22}O_{11}$?
   a. 11   b. **22**   c. 22   d. 45
6. Which of the following is a compound?
   a. iron   b. blood   c. **carbon dioxide**   d. air
7. A(n) _____ contains two or more atoms bonded together.
   a. mixture   b. **molecule**   c. atom   d. element
8. A substance that contains two or more different kinds of atoms bonded together is _____.
   a. an element   b. oxygen   c. energy   d. **a compound**
9. How many atoms of oxygen are represented in the equation: $C + O_2 \rightarrow CO_2$?
   a. 1   b. **2**   c. 3   d. 4
10. The smallest part of a compound that still has the properties of that compound is a(n) _____.
    a. atom   b. cell   c. **molecule**   d. element
11. An atom that contains 15 protons and 10 neutrons within its nucleus will have an atomic mass of _____ amu.
    a. 5   b. 10   c. 15   d. **25**
12. An atom of atomic number 12 and mass number 22 contains how many protons?
    a. 10   b. **12**   c. 22   d. 34
13. The atom described in problem 12 will have how many electrons?
    a. 10   b. **12**   c. 22   d. 34
14. The atom described in problem 12 will have how many neutrons?
    a. **10**   b. 12   c. 22   d. 34
15. Elements combine by losing, sharing, or gaining _____.
    a. **electrons**   b. protons   c. neutrons   d. molecules

15

Acid, Base, or Salt?

Classify each as an *acid*, a *base*, or a *salt*.

1. HNO_3 — **acid**
2. $NaOH$ — **base**
3. $NaNO_3$ — **salt**
4. HCl — **acid**
5. KCl — **salt**
6. $Ba(OH)_2$ — **base**
7. KOH — **base**
8. H_2S — **acid**
9. $Al(NO_3)_3$ — **salt**
10. H_2SO_4 — **acid**
11. $CaCl_2$ — **salt**
12. H_3PO_4 — **acid**
13. Na_2SO_4 — **salt**
14. $Mg(OH)_2$ — **base**
15. H_2CO_3 — **acid**
16. NH_4OH — **base**
17. NH_4Cl — **salt**
18. HBr — **acid**
19. $FeBr_3$ — **salt**
20. HF — **acid**
21. $NaCl$ — **salt**
22. $Ca(OH)_2$ — **base**
23. $HC_2H_3O_2$ — **acid**
24. $CuCl_2$ — **salt**
25. HNO_2 — **acid**

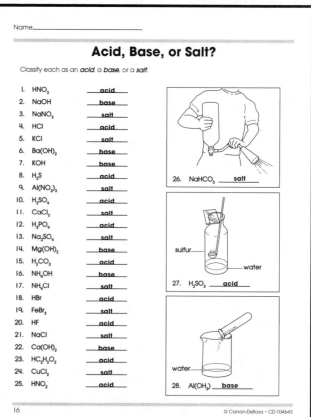

26. $NaHCO_3$ — **salt**

27. H_2SO_3 — **acid**

sulfur

water

water

28. $Al(OH)_3$ — **base**

16

Answer Key

Name_____

pH

pH is a scale that measures the hydronium ion concentration of a solution. A pH of less than 7 indicates an acidic solution. A solution with a pH of 7 is neutral. A solution with a pH of 7 to 14 is basic and contains a higher concentration of hydroxide ions than hydronium ions.

Indicators are substances that change color in the presence of certain ions. Phenolphthalein is colorless in acids and neutral solutions, but pink in a base. Litmus is red in an acid and blue in a base.

For each substance, indicate the pH range expected. Indicate the color the indicator will appear and state the solution's use.

Solution	pH Range	Phenolphtalein	Blue Litmus	Red Litmus	Use
vinegar	< 7	colorless	red	red	pickling
soap	> 7	pink	blue	blue	cleaning
cola	< 7	colorless	red	red	drinking, digestion
ammonia	> 7	pink	blue	blue	cleaning
rain	< 7	colorless	red	red	replenishing water, continues water cycle
milk	< 7	colorless	red	red	provides calcium
saliva	< 7	colorless	red	red	begins digestion of carbohydrates
coffee	< 7	colorless	red	red	drinking
gastric juices	< 7	colorless	red	red	breaking down food
human blood	> 7	pink	blue	blue	transporting oxygen
orange juice	< 7	colorless	red	red	nutrition
drain cleaner	> 7	pink	blue	blue	dissolving oil, soap, etc.
bleach	> 7	pink	blue	blue	killing bacteria, whitening
shampoo	< 7	colorless	red	red	cleaning, dissolving oils

© Carson-Dellosa • CD-104643   17

Name_____

Inorganic vs. Organic Compounds

Matter is often classified as organic or inorganic. Indicate the class for each type of matter as *organic* or *inorganic*. Then, identify its major properties as that of a *salt, acid, base, protein, lipid, nucleic acid,* or *carbohydrate*.

	Matter	Class	Properties of
1.	HCl	inorganic	acid
2.	DNA	organic	nucleic acid
3.	starch	organic	carbohydrate
4.	KOH	inorganic	base
5.	sodium chloride	inorganic	salt
6.	skin	organic	protein
7.	animal fat	organic	lipid
8.	glucose	organic	carbohydrate
9.	vegetable oil	organic	lipid
10.	hair	organic	protein
11.	RNA	organic	nucleic acid
12.	sucrose	organic	carbohydrate
13.	butter	organic	lipid
14.	fingernails	organic	protein
15.	H_2SO_4	inorganic	acid
16.	HNO_3	inorganic	acid
17.	gelatin	organic	protein
18.	molasses	organic	carbohydrate
19.	vinegar	organic	acid

18   © Carson-Dellosa • CD-104643

Name_____

Dehydration Synthesis

In each example of dehydration synthesis, show how the removal of the water molecule(s) takes place by drawing a box around the components of water. Then, draw the structural formula of each product.

Synthesis of a Fat

Formation of a Peptide Bond

Name_____

Hydrolysis

Hydrolysis is the opposite of a dehydration synthesis. A large molecule is broken down into two or more smaller molecules by the addition of water.

Draw the structural formulas of the expected products in each hydrolysis reaction.

Breakdown of a Disaccharide to Monosaccharides

Breakdown of a Lipid

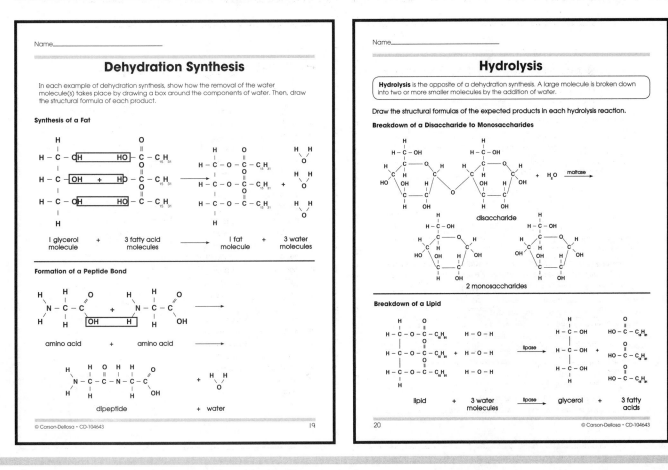

© Carson-Dellosa • CD-104643   19

20   © Carson-Dellosa • CD-104643

Answer Key

Diffusion and Osmosis

The diagrams show what each solution would look like after a period of time has passed. Then, label each as *osmosis* or *diffusion*.

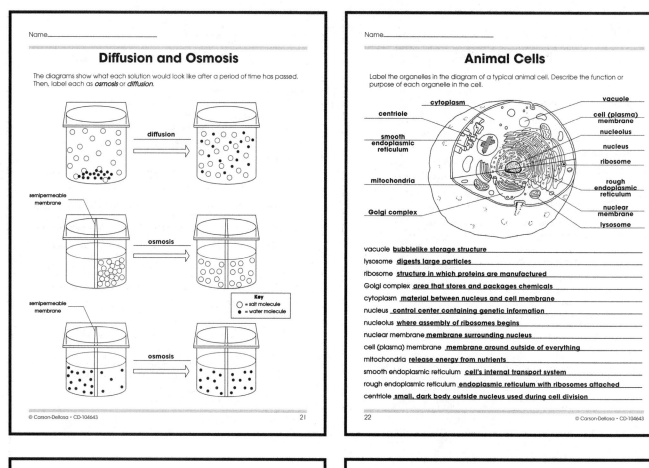

Animal Cells

Label the organelles in the diagram of a typical animal cell. Describe the function or purpose of each organelle in the cell.

vacuole **bubblelike storage structure**

lysosome **digests large particles**

ribosome **structure in which proteins are manufactured**

Golgi complex **area that stores and packages chemicals**

cytoplasm **material between nucleus and cell membrane**

nucleus **control center containing genetic information**

nucleolus **where assembly of ribosomes begins**

nuclear membrane **membrane surrounding nucleus**

cell (plasma) membrane **membrane around outside of everything**

mitochondria **release energy from nutrients**

smooth endoplasmic reticulum **cell's internal transport system**

rough endoplasmic reticulum **endoplasmic reticulum with ribosomes attached**

centriole **small, dark body outside nucleus used during cell division**

Plant Cells

Label the organelles in the diagram of a typical plant cell. Describe the function or purpose of each organelle in the cell.

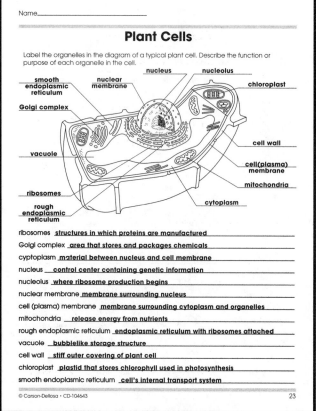

ribosomes **structures in which proteins are manufactured**

Golgi complex **area that stores and packages chemicals**

cyptoplasm **material between nucleus and cell membrane**

nucleus **control center containing genetic information**

nucleolus **where ribosome production begins**

nuclear membrane **membrane surrounding nucleus**

cell (plasma) membrane **membrane surrounding cytoplasm and organelles**

mitochondria **release energy from nutrients**

rough endoplasmic reticulum **endoplasmic reticulum with ribosomes attached**

vacuole **bubblelike storage structure**

cell wall **stiff outer covering of plant cell**

chloroplast **plastid that stores chlorophyll used in photosynthesis**

smooth endoplasmic reticulum **cell's internal transport system**

Function of the Organelles

Identify the organelle that performs each function within the cell.

	Function	Organelle
1.	Controls the movement into and out of the cell	cell (plasma) membrane
2.	Watery material that contains many of the materials involved in cell metabolism	cytoplasm
3.	Serves as a pathway for the transport of materials throughout the cell; also associated with synthesis and storage	endoplasmic reticulum
4.	Serves as the control center for cell metabolism and reproduction	nucleus
5.	Sites of protein synthesis	ribosomes
6.	Involved in the digestion of food within the cell	lysosomes
7.	The "powerhouse" of the cell	mitochondria
8.	Packages and secretes the products of the cell	Golgi apparatus
9.	Involved in cell division in animal cells	centrioles
10.	Fluid filled organelles enclosed by a membrane; contains stored food or wastes	vacuoles
11.	Site of the production of ribosomes	nucleolus
12.	Controls movement into and out of the nucleus	nuclear membrane
13.	Gives the cell its shape and provides protection; not found in animal cells	cell wall
14.	Hairlike structures with the capacity for movement	cilia
15.	A long, hairlike structure used for movement	flagellum
16.	Site of photosynthesis	chloroplast
17.	During cytokinesis, the new cell wall that begins to form in the middle, dividing the two sides	cell plate
18.	Rod-shaped bodies that carry genetic information	chromosomes

Answer Key

Name_____

Parts of the Cell

Match each description with the appropriate term.

g	1. holds nucleus together		a.	Golgi bodies
f	2. surface for chemical activity		b.	nucleus
p	3. units of heredity		c.	chromosomes
o	4. digestion center		d.	vacuole
e	5. where proteins are made		e.	ribosomes
h	6. structures involved in mitosis in animal cells		f.	endoplasmic reticulum
t	7. microscopic cylinders that support and give the cell shape		g.	nuclear membrane
m	8. shapes and supports a plant cell		h.	centrioles
a	9. stores and releases chemicals		i.	cytoplasm
k	10. food for plant cells is made here		j.	chlorophyll
r	11. spherical body within nucleus		k.	chloroplasts
l	12. controls entry into and out of cell		l.	cell (plasma) membrane
j	13. traps light and is used to produce food for plants		m.	cell wall
b	14. chromosomes are found here		n.	mitochondria
i	15. jellylike substance within cell		o.	lysosome
c	16. contains code that guides all cell activity		p.	genes
q	17. minute hole in the nuclear membrane		q.	nuclear pore
n	18. "powerhouse" of cell		r.	nucleolus
d	19. contains water and dissolved minerals		s.	plastid
s	20. stores food or contains pigment		t.	microtubule

Name_____

Cellular Respiration

Complete each sequence.

Glycolysis

glucose + __**2**__ ATP $\xrightarrow{\text{enzymes}}$ 2 __**pyruvic acid**__ + __**4**__ ATP

Anaerobic Respiration

2 pyruvic acid $\longrightarrow$ 2 __**lactic acid**__

or

2 pyruvic acid $\longrightarrow$ 2 __**alcohol**__ + 2 __**carbon dioxide**__

Aerobic Respiration

2 pyruvic acid + oxygen $\xrightarrow{\text{enzymes}}$ __**carbon dioxide**__ + __**water**__ + __**34**__ ATP

Complete each sentence.

1. Glycolysis produces a net gain of __**2**__ ATP molecules per molecule of glucose by an anaerobic reaction.

2. Aerobic respiration produces a net gain of __**34**__ ATP molecules per molecule of glucose.

3. __**Aerobic**__ respiration is a more efficient producer of energy than anaerobic respiration.

4. The energy contained in a molecule of glucose is changed to a more usable form by combining a __**phosphorous**__ atom with __**ADP**__ to form ATP.

5. When ATP is broken down to __**ADP**__ and __**phosphorous**__, energy is __**released**__.

6. During glycolysis, glucose is first split into two molecules of __**PGAL**__. This requires the energy released from two molecules of ATP being converted to two molecules of __**ADP**__.

7. The __**PGAL**__ is then converted to __**pyruvic acid**__, producing four __**ADP**__ molecules and two __**ADP**__ molecules, which are part of the electron transport chain.

8. The __**electron**__ transport chain, which supplies the energy needed for the formation of ATP, requires the formation of __**NADH**__ from NAD⁺, and __**FADH₂**__ from FAD.

9. The hydrogen necessary in this chain comes from the breaking apart of __**water**__ molecules.

10. The oxygen released is used to form __**CO₂**__.

Name_____

Stages of Mitosis

Label each diagram of a stage of mitosis in an animal cell with the proper number and name.

1. prophase   5. daughter cells   3. anaphase

6. interphase   2. metaphase   4. telophase

Label each diagram of mitosis in a plant cell with the proper number and name.

5. daughter cells   1. prophase   3. anaphase

2. metaphase   6. interphase   4. telophase

Name_____

Stages of Meiosis

Number the diagrams of a first meiotic division in the proper order. Label each phase as *prophase I, metaphase I, anaphase I,* or *telophase I.*

2. metaphase I   1. prophase I   3. anaphase I   4. telophase I

Number the diagrams of the second meiotic division. Label each phase as *prophase II, metaphase II, anaphase II,* or *telophase II.*

1. prophase II   4. telophase II   3. anaphase II   2. metaphase II

Answer Key

Name_____

Comparing Mitosis and Meiosis

Determine whether each characteristic applies to mitosis, meiosis, or both by putting a check in the appropriate column(s).

		Mitosis	Meiosis
1.	no pairing of homologs occurs	✓	
2.	two divisions		✓
3.	four daughter cells produced		✓
4.	associated with growth and asexual reproduction	✓	
5.	associated with sexual reproduction		✓
6.	one division	✓	
7.	two daughter cells produced	✓	
8.	involves duplication of chromosomes	✓	✓
9.	chromosome number is maintained	✓	
10.	chromosome number is halved		✓
11.	crossing over between homologous chromosomes may occur		✓
12.	daughter cells are identical to parent cell	✓	
13.	daughter cells are not identical to parent cell		✓
14.	produces gametes		✓
15.	synopsis occurs in prophase		✓

Name_____

Types of Asexual Reproduction

Label the diagrams of types of asexual reproduction as *binary fission*, *budding*, *parthenogenesis*, *regeneration*, *sporulation*, or *vegetative propagation*.

Type _____**binary fission**_____
Examples _____**bacteria**_____
_____**amoeba**_____

Type _____**budding**_____
Examples _____**yeast**_____
_____**hydra**_____

Type _____**sporulation**_____
Examples _____**bread mold**_____
_____**moss**_____

Type _____**regeneration**_____
Examples _____**starfish**_____
_____**sponge**_____

Type _____**parthenogenesis**_____
Examples _____**Daphina**_____
_____**aphids**_____

Type _____**vegetative propagation**_____
Examples _____**potatoes**_____
_____**strawberries**_____

Name_____

Classification

Number the seven major classification groups in order from the one containing the largest number of organisms to that containing the least.

__4__	order	__2__	phylum
__5__	family	__7__	species
__1__	kingdom	__3__	class
__6__	genus		

On the chart, classify the five kingdoms according to the characteristics in the left-hand column.

Characteristics	Monera	Protista	Fungi	Plantae	Animalia
cell type (prokaryotic/ eukaryotic)	prokaryotic	eukaryotic	eukaryotic	eukaryotic	eukaryotic
number of cells (unicellular/ multicellular)	unicellular	multi-cellular	multi-cellular	multi-cellular	multi-cellular
cell nucleus (present/absent)	absent	present	present	present	present
cell wall (present/absent)	present	present in some	present	present	present
cell wall composition	poly-saccharides, amino acids	varies	chitin	cellulose	—
nutrition (autotrophic/ heterotrophic)	both	both	hetero-trophic	auto-trophic	hetero-trophic
locomotion (present/absent)	present in some	present in some	absent	absent	absent

---

Name_____

Classifying Organisms

Give the name of each organism and indicate the phylum to which it belongs.

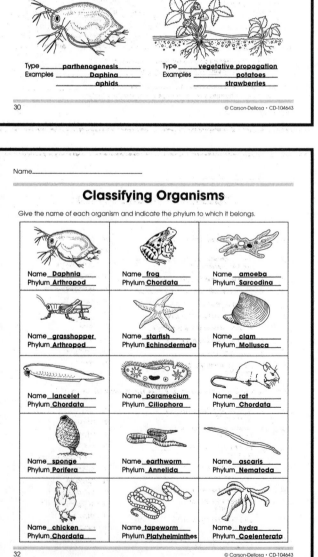

Name **Daphnia**
Phylum **Arthropod**

Name **frog**
Phylum **Chordata**

Name **amoeba**
Phylum **Sarcodina**

Name **grasshopper**
Phylum **Arthropod**

Name **starfish**
Phylum **Echinodermata**

Name **clam**
Phylum **Mollusca**

Name **lancelet**
Phylum **Chordata**

Name **paramecium**
Phylum **Ciliophora**

Name **rat**
Phylum **Chordata**

Name **sponge**
Phylum **Porifera**

Name **earthworm**
Phylum **Annelida**

Name **ascaris**
Phylum **Nematoda**

Name **chicken**
Phylum **Chordata**

Name **tapeworm**
Phylum **Platyhelminthes**

Name **hydra**
Phylum **Coelenterata**

Answer Key

Name_____

Nutrition in Protozoans

Label the parts on the diagram of an amoeba. State the function or purpose of each part.

a. food vacuole **used for digestion and temporary storage**
b. pseudopods **temporary footlike projection used in locomotion**
c. nucleus **control center of cell**
d. contractile vacuole **gets rid of excess water and waste**
e. cell membrane **outside boundary of the cell**
f. ectoplasm **the layer of cytoplasm under the cell membrane**
g. endoplasm **the cytoplasm that fills the cell**

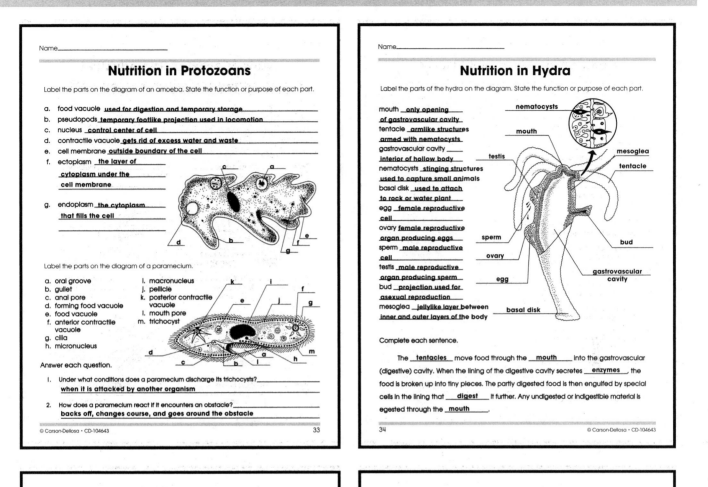

Label the parts on the diagram of a paramecium.

a. oral groove
b. gullet
c. anal pore
d. forming food vacuole
e. food vacuole
f. anterior contractile vacuole
g. cilia
h. micronucleus
i. macronucleus
j. pellicle
k. posterior contractile vacuole
l. mouth pore
m. trichocyst

Answer each question.

1. Under what conditions does a paramecium discharge its trichocysts?
   when it is attacked by another organism

2. How does a paramecium react if it encounters an obstacle?
   backs off, changes course, and goes around the obstacle

© Carson-Dellosa • CD-104643   33

Name_____

Nutrition in Hydra

Label the parts of the hydra on the diagram. State the function or purpose of each part.

mouth **only opening of gastrovascular cavity**
tentacle **armlike structures armed with nematocysts**
gastrovascular cavity **interior of hollow body**
nematocysts **stinging structures used to capture small animals**
basal disk **used to attach to rock or water plant**
egg **female reproductive cell**
ovary **female reproductive organ producing eggs**
sperm **male reproductive cell**
testis **male reproductive organ producing sperm**
bud **projection used for asexual reproduction**
mesoglea **jellylike layer between inner and outer layers of the body**

Complete each sentence.

The **tentacles** move food through the **mouth** into the gastrovascular (digestive) cavity. When the lining of the digestive cavity secretes **enzymes**, the food is broken up into tiny pieces. The partly digested food is then engulfed by special cells in the lining that **digest** it further. Any undigested or indigestible material is egested through the **mouth**.

34   © Carson-Dellosa • CD-104643

Name_____

Classification and Protists

Match the definition with the correct word. Not all words will be used.

c 1. method of sexual reproduction in paramecia
e 2. protozoan with short, hairlike structures used for movement
a 3. fingerlike projections of cytoplasm
d 4. protozoan with a three-stage life cycle
k 5. largest category in a kingdom
b 6. first word in a scientific name
j 7. science of classifying living things
i 8. smallest category in a kingdom
f 9. division of a class
h 10. method of reproduction in an amoeba

a. pseudopod
b. genus
c. conjugation
d. slime mold
e. paramecium
f. order
g. class
h. fission
i. species
j. taxonomy
k. phylum

Match the functions to the correct organelle. Not all words will be used.

f 11. gives shape to the paramecium and euglena
c 12. controls sexual reproduction in the paramecium
e 13. used for excretion of waste products
b 14. contains chlorophyll
i 15. reacts to light
g 16. used for movement by euglena
k 17. controls metabolism of a paramecium
a 18. used for movement by a paramecium
d 19. The paramecium ingests its food through this opening.

a. cilia
b. chloroplast
c. micronucleus
d. oral groove
e. contractile vacuole
f. pellicle
g. flagellum
h. cytostome
i. eyespot
j. pseudopod
k. macronucleus

© Carson-Dellosa • CD-104643   35

Name_____

Self Quiz: Classification and Protists

Circle the letter of the correct answer.

1. Of the following groups, a _____ contains animals that are least alike.
   a. family   **b. phylum**   c. division   d. class
2. Which of the following groupings contain the most closely related organisms?
   a. family   b. phylum   **c. genus**   d. kingdom
3. Which of the following is a correctly written scientific name?
   a. Panthera Leo   b. panthera leo   c. PANTHERA LEO   **d. Panthera leo**
4. The smallest category of a kingdom is a(n) _____.
   a. division   **b. species**   c. phylum   d. genus
5. _____ is the science of classifying living things.
   a. Astronomy   b. Biology   **c. Taxonomy**   d. Zoology
6. The cat and dog belong to the same order but different _____.
   a. kingdoms   b. classes   **c. families**   d. divisions
7. Living things are usually classified into five _____.
   a. phyla   **b. kingdoms**   c. classes   d. divisions
8. Which of the following is a Felis domesticus?
   a. horse   **b. house cat**   c. house finch   d. lion
9. What language is used for scientific names?
   a. English   b. Swedish   c. German   **d. Latin**
10. Organisms are classified into the group with which they share the greatest number of _____.
    a. food   b. territory   **c. characteristics**   d. time
11. Why does each organism have a specific scientific name?
    a. for study and communication   c. name contains important information
    b. classification is less involved   d. easier to alphabetize all organisms
12. Protozoans and slime molds belong to a group of organisms known as _____.
    a. protists   b. fungi   c. lichens   d. parasites
13. The fingerlike projections of cytoplasm used by some protozoans for movement and obtaining food are:
    a. hyphae   b. sporangia   **c. pseudopods**   d. oral grooves
14. A protist that has chlorophyll and produces its own food is a(n) _____ protist.
    a. plantlike   b. sporozoan   c. animallike   d. saprophyte
15. A protist covered with many short hairlike structures used for movement is a _____.
    a. parasite   **b. ciliate**   c. flagellate   d. lichen
16. Which of the following protists have shells made of silica?
    a. diatoms   b. ciliates   c. amoeba   d. paramecia
17. The kingdom with one-celled organisms that are plantlike, animallike, and funguslike is _____.
    a. amoeba   b. protozoa   **c. protista**   d. fungi
18. The long, hairlike structures protists use for locomotion are _____.
    a. cilia   **b. flagella**   c. pseudopods   d. trichocysts

36   © Carson-Dellosa • CD-104643

Answer Key

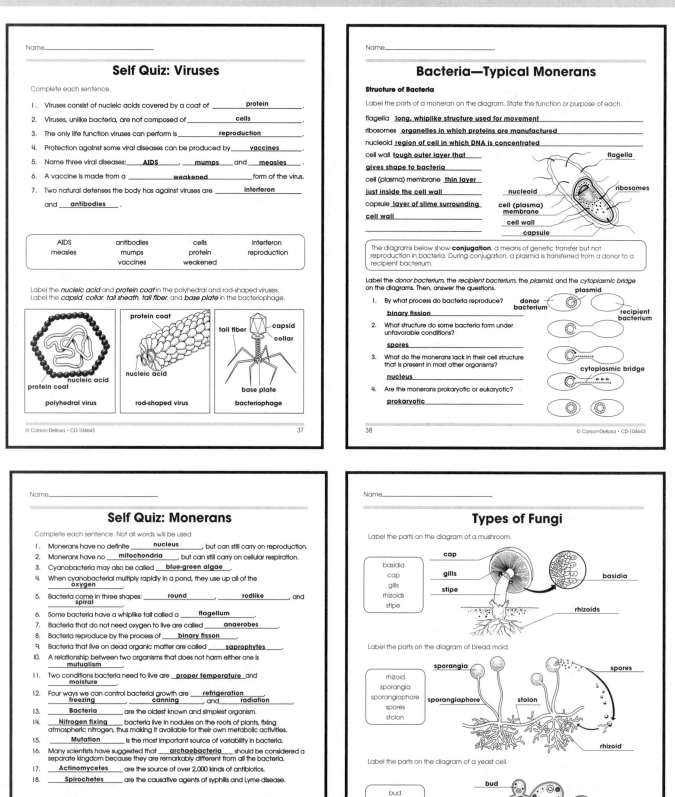

Self Quiz: Viruses

Complete each sentence.

1. Viruses consist of nucleic acids covered by a coat of **protein**.
2. Viruses, unlike bacteria, are not composed of **cells**.
3. The only life function viruses can perform is **reproduction**.
4. Protection against some viral diseases can be produced by **vaccines**.
5. Name three viral diseases: **AIDS**, **mumps** and **measles**.
6. A vaccine is made from a **weakened** form of the virus.
7. Two natural defenses the body has against viruses are **interferon** and **antibodies**.

AIDS	antibodies	cells	interferon
measles	mumps	protein	reproduction
	vaccines	weakened	

Label the *nucleic acid* and *protein coat* in the polyhedral and rod-shaped viruses.
Label the *capsid, collar, tail sheath, tail fiber,* and *base plate* in the bacteriophage.

protein coat
nucleic acid
protein coat
polyhedral virus

protein coat
nucleic acid
rod-shaped virus

tail fiber
capsid
collar
base plate
bacteriophage

© Carson-Dellosa • CD-104643   37

Bacteria—Typical Monerans

Structure of Bacteria

Label the parts of a moneran on the diagram. State the function or purpose of each.

flagella **long, whiplike structure used for movement**
ribosomes **organelles in which proteins are manufactured**
nucleoid **region of cell in which DNA is concentrated**
cell wall **tough outer layer that gives shape to bacteria**
cell (plasma) membrane **thin layer just inside the cell wall**
capsule **layer of slime surrounding cell wall**

flagella
ribosomes
nucleoid
cell (plasma) membrane
cell wall
capsule

The diagrams below show **conjugation**, a means of genetic transfer but not reproduction in bacteria. During conjugation, a plasmid is transferred from a donor to a recipient bacterium.

Label the *donor bacterium,* the *recipient bacterium,* the *plasmid,* and the *cytoplasmic bridge* on the diagrams. Then, answer the questions.

1. By what process do bacteria reproduce?
   binary fission
2. What structure do some bacteria form under unfavorable conditions?
   spores
3. What do the monerans lack in their cell structure that is present in most other organisms?
   nucleus
4. Are the monerans prokaryotic or eukaryotic?
   prokaryotic

plasmid
donor bacterium
recipient bacterium
cytoplasmic bridge

38   © Carson-Dellosa • CD-104643

Self Quiz: Monerans

Complete each sentence. Not all words will be used

1. Monerans have no definite **nucleus**, but can still carry on reproduction.
2. Monerans have no **mitochondria**, but can still carry on cellular respiration.
3. Cyanobacteria may also be called **blue-green algae**.
4. When cyanobacteria multiply rapidly in a pond, they use up all of the **oxygen**.
5. Bacteria come in three shapes: **round**, **rodlike**, and **spiral**.
6. Some bacteria have a whiplike tail called a **flagellum**.
7. Bacteria that do not need oxygen to live are called **anaerobes**.
8. Bacteria reproduce by the process of **binary fisson**.
9. Bacteria that live on dead organic matter are called **saprophytes**.
10. A relationship between two organisms that does not harm either one is **mutualism**.
11. Two conditions bacteria need to live are **proper temperature** and **moisture**.
12. Four ways we can control bacterial growth are **refrigeration**, **freezing**, **canning**, and **radiation**.
13. **Bacteria** are the oldest known and simplest organism.
14. **Nitrogen fixing** bacteria live in nodules on the roots of plants, fixing atmospheric nitrogen, thus making it available for their own metabolic activities.
15. **Mutation** is the most important source of variability in bacteria.
16. Many scientists have suggested that **archaebacteria** should be considered a separate kingdom because they are remarkably different from all the rest.
17. **Actinomycetes** are the source of over 2,000 kinds of antibiotics.
18. **Spirochetes** are the causative agents of syphilis and Lyme disease.

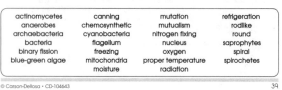

actinomycetes	canning	mutation	refrigeration
anaerobes	chemosynthetic	mutualism	rodlike
archaebacteria	cyanobacteria	nitrogen fixing	round
bacteria	flagellum	nucleus	saprophytes
binary fission	freezing	oxygen	spiral
blue-green algae	mitochondria	proper temperature	spirochetes
	moisture	radiation	

© Carson-Dellosa • CD-104643   39

Types of Fungi

Label the parts on the diagram of a mushroom.

| basidia |
| cap |
| gills |
| rhizoids |
| stipe |

cap
gills
stipe
basidia
rhizoids

Label the parts on the diagram of bread mold.

| rhizoid |
| sporangia |
| sporangiophore |
| spores |
| stolon |

sporangia
spores
sporangiaphore
stolon
rhizoid

Label the parts on the diagram of a yeast cell.

| bud |
| cell wall |
| cytoplasm |
| nucleus |
| vacuole |

bud
cell wall
nucleus
cytoplasm
vacuole

40   © Carson-Dellosa • CD-104643

Answer Key

Self Quiz: Fungi

Circle the letter of the correct answer.

1. During the process of _____, energy is released.
   a. parasitism b. fermentation c. mutualism d. reproduction
2. _____ are saclike structures that produce many spores.
   a. Pseudopods b. Gilla **c.** Sporangia d. Hyphae
3. Club fungi produce spores on a sac called a(n) _____.
   a. bud b. basidium **c.** ascus d. stripe
4. Bread mold produces masses of threadlike structures called_____.
   a. flagella b. cilia **c.** hyphae d. pseudopods
5. _____ are fungi that produce spores in special structures on the tips of hyphae.
   a. Yeasts b. Lichens c. Mushrooms **d.** Sporangia fungi
6. _____ is a type of sexual reproduction in which an outgrowth from the parent organism forms a new organism.
   a. Budding b. Zygospore c. Sporangia d. Basidia
7. Sac fungi are fungi that _____.
   a. look like mosses c. are helpful because they produce enzymes
   b. are one-celled **d.** produce spores inside an ascus
8. Yeast cells may reproduce by forming spores or by _____.
   a. fermentation **b.** budding c. respiration d. dehydration
9. A sporangium fungus obtains food by _____.
   a. respiration b. dehydration **c.** absorption d. mutualism
10. Club fungi include puffballs, bracken fungi, and _____.
    a. molds b. yeasts **c.** mushrooms d. lichens
11. A sporangium fungus reproduces by _____.
    a. budding and spores c. anaerobic respiration
    b. spores and zygospores d. a micronucleus
12. Unlike a plant, a fungus does not have _____.
    a. very many cells **b.** chlorophyll
    c. cell walls d. buds
13. Which one of the following helpful fungi is used to flavor cheese?
    a. mushrooms b. saprophytic fungi c. yeast **d.** molds
14. Each basidium will produce how many spores?
    a. thousands b. hundreds **c.** four d. ten
15. The basidia are found on what part of the mushroom?
    a. stipe **b.** gills c. cap d. hyphae
16. Fermentation produces what products?
    a. alcohol and carbon dioxide c. alcohol and water
    b. air bubbles and sugar d. carbon dioxide and sugar
17. Masses of hyphae are called _____.
    a. basidia b. sporangia **c.** mycelium d. asci
18. Another name for anaerobic respiration in fungi is _____.
    a. budding b. reproduction c. breathing **d.** fermentation
19. A person who studies fungi is called a _____.
    a. fungicide **b.** mycologist c. zygospore d. saprophyte
20. The cell walls of fungi are made of _____.
    a. cellulose **b.** chitin c. silica d. tissue

41

Autotrophs vs. Heterotrophs

An **autotroph** is an organism that is capable of forming organic compounds from inorganic compounds in its environment. In other words, an autotroph can make its own food. **Heterotrophs** must get their food from other organisms.

Classify each organism as an autotroph (A) or a heterotroph (H).

1. maple tree   **A**
2. human   **H**
3. wheat   **A**
4. fungi   **H**
5. amoeba   **H**
6. green algae   **A**
7. house fly   **H**
8. fern   **A**
9. dandelion   **A**
10. goldfish   **H**

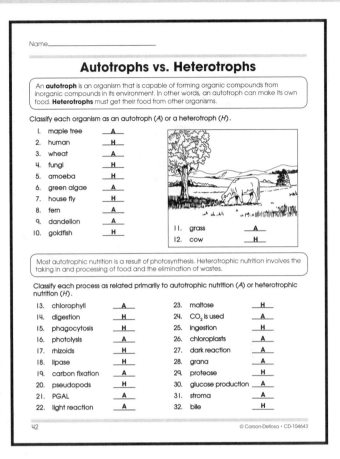

11. grass   **A**
12. cow   **H**

Most autotrophic nutrition is a result of photosynthesis. Heterotrophic nutrition involves the taking in and processing of food and the elimination of wastes.

Classify each process as related primarily to autotrophic nutrition (A) or heterotrophic nutrition (H).

13. chlorophyll   **A**
14. digestion   **H**
15. phagocytosis   **H**
16. photolysis   **A**
17. rhizoids   **H**
18. lipase   **H**
19. carbon fixation   **A**
20. pseudopods   **H**
21. PGAL   **A**
22. light reaction   **A**
23. maltose   **H**
24. CO_2 is used   **A**
25. ingestion   **H**
26. chloroplasts   **A**
27. dark reaction   **A**
28. grana   **A**
29. proteose   **H**
30. glucose production   **A**
31. stroma   **A**
32. bile   **H**

42

Cross Section of a Leaf

Label the parts of the leaf in the diagram. Give the purpose or function of each part.

lower epidermis **outmost tissue on lower side of leaf**

upper epidermis **outmost tissue on upper side of leaf**

palisade layer **row of elongated cells in upper center leaf**

cuticle **waxy substance covering the epidermis**

stomata **opening between two guard cells on lower side of leaf**

guard cells **two sausage-shaped cells surrounding each stomata**

vein (fibrovascular bundle) **supplies structural support; contains xylem and phloem**

spongy layer **irregularly shaped cells in lower center of leaf**

air space **space in the spongy layer; contains gases**

xylem **transfers water and minerals to cells of the leaf**

phloem **transports products of photosynthesis from leaf to rest of the plant**

chloroplasts **cells containing chlorophyll**

mesophyll **middle tissue of a leaf**

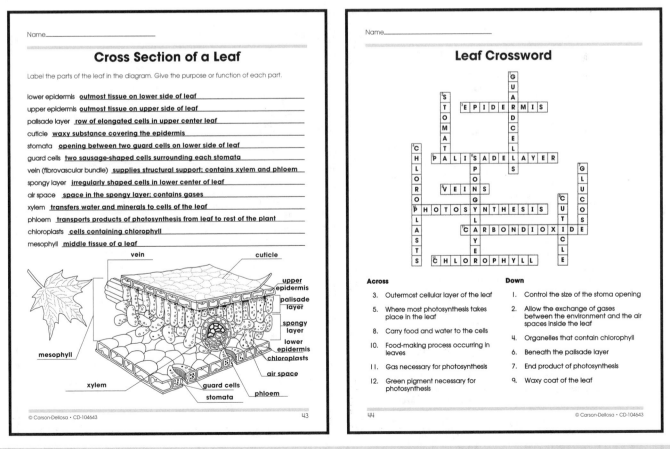

43

Leaf Crossword

Across

3. Outermost cellular layer of the leaf

5. Where most photosynthesis takes place in the leaf

8. Carry food and water to the cells

10. Food-making process occurring in leaves

11. Gas necessary for photosynthesis

12. Green pigment necessary for photosynthesis

Down

1. Control the size of the stoma opening

2. Allow the exchange of gases between the environment and the air spaces inside the leaf

4. Organelles that contain chlorophyll

6. Beneath the palisade layer

7. End product of photosynthesis

9. Waxy coat of the leaf

44

Answer Key

Name_____

Structure of a Root

Label the parts on the diagrams of a cross section and longitudinal section of a root.

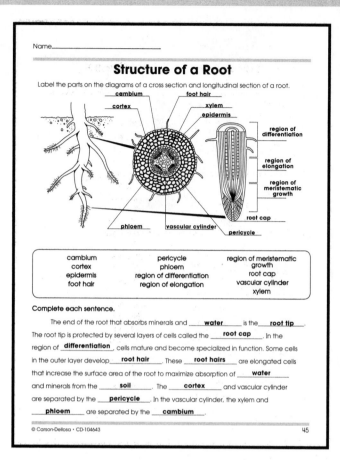

Complete each sentence.

The end of the root that absorbs minerals and **water** is the **root tip**. The root tip is protected by several layers of cells called the **root cap**. In the region of **differentiation**, cells mature and become specialized in function. Some cells in the outer layer develop **root hair**. These **root hairs** are elongated cells that increase the surface area of the root to maximize absorption of **water** and minerals from the **soil**. The **cortex** and vascular cylinder are separated by the **pericycle**. In the vascular cylinder, the xylem and **phloem** are separated by the **cambium**.

© Carson-Dellosa • CD-104643

45

Name_____

Structure of a Flower

Label the parts of a flower in the diagram. Give the purpose or function of each part.

ovary   **swollen base of pistil**

style   **slender middle portion of pistil**

stigma   **sticky tip at top of style**

sepal   **leaflike structure that encloses the flower bud**

receptacle   **base of flower**

pedicel   **stalk on which flower rests**

petal   **modified, colored leaf of flower**

filament   **thin, stemlike part of the stamen**

anther   **upper portion of stamen in which pollen is produced**

pollen grain   **fertilizing element of flower**

pistil   **female part ef flower**

stamen   **male part of flower**

ovule   **part of ovary in which eggs are produced**

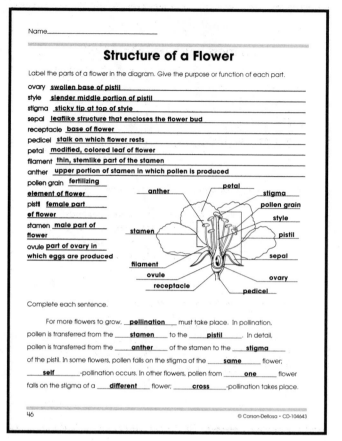

Complete each sentence.

For more flowers to grow, **pollination** must take place. In pollination, pollen is transferred from the **stamen** to the **pistil**. In detail, pollen is transferred from the **anther** of the stamen to the **stigma** of the pistil. In some flowers, pollen falls on the stigma of the **same** flower; **self**-pollination occurs. In other flowers, pollen from **one** flower falls on the stigma of a **different** flower; **cross**-pollination takes place.

46

© Carson-Dellosa • CD-104643

Name_____

Structure of the Stamen and Pollen

Label the parts on the diagrams of double fertilization in a flower.

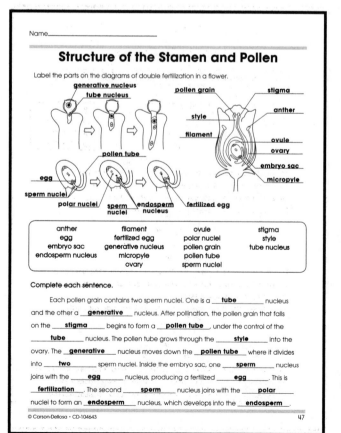

Complete each sentence.

Each pollen grain contains two sperm nuclei. One is a **tube** nucleus and the other a **generative** nucleus. After pollination, the pollen grain that falls on the **stigma** begins to form a **pollen tube**, under the control of the **tube** nucleus. The pollen tube grows through the **style** into the ovary. The **generative** nucleus moves down the **pollen tube** where it divides into **two** sperm nuclei. Inside the embryo sac, one **sperm** nucleus joins with the **egg** nucleus, producing a fertilized **egg**. This is **fertilization**. The second **sperm** nucleus joins with the **polar** nuclei to form an **endosperm** nucleus, which develops into the **endosperm**.

© Carson-Dellosa • CD-104643

47

Name_____

Ecological Relationships

Use the food web to answer each question.

1. When the hawk is the third-order consumer, the number of second-order consumers shown is **five**.

2. The food chain that includes insect-eating birds is **shrubs, insects, birds, and hawks**.

3. The animal that consumes the largest number of different types of first-order and second-order consumers is the **hawk**.

4. All of the animals that are herbivores are **first-order** consumers.

5. If no snakes were in the food web, the squirrels and rabbits could still be eaten by the **hawks**.

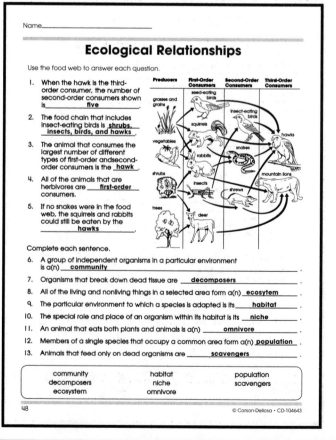

Complete each sentence.

6. A group of independent organisms in a particular environment is a(n) **community**.

7. Organisms that break down dead tissue are **decomposers**.

8. All of the living and nonliving things in a selected area form a(n) **ecosytem**.

9. The particular environment to which a species is adapted is its **habitat**.

10. The special role and place of an organism within its habitat is its **niche**.

11. An animal that eats both plants and animals is a(n) **omnivore**.

12. Members of a single species that occupy a common area form a(n) **population**.

13. Animals that feed only on dead organisms are **scavengers**.

community	habitat	population
decomposers	niche	scavengers
ecosystem	omnivore	

48

© Carson-Dellosa • CD-104643

Answer Key

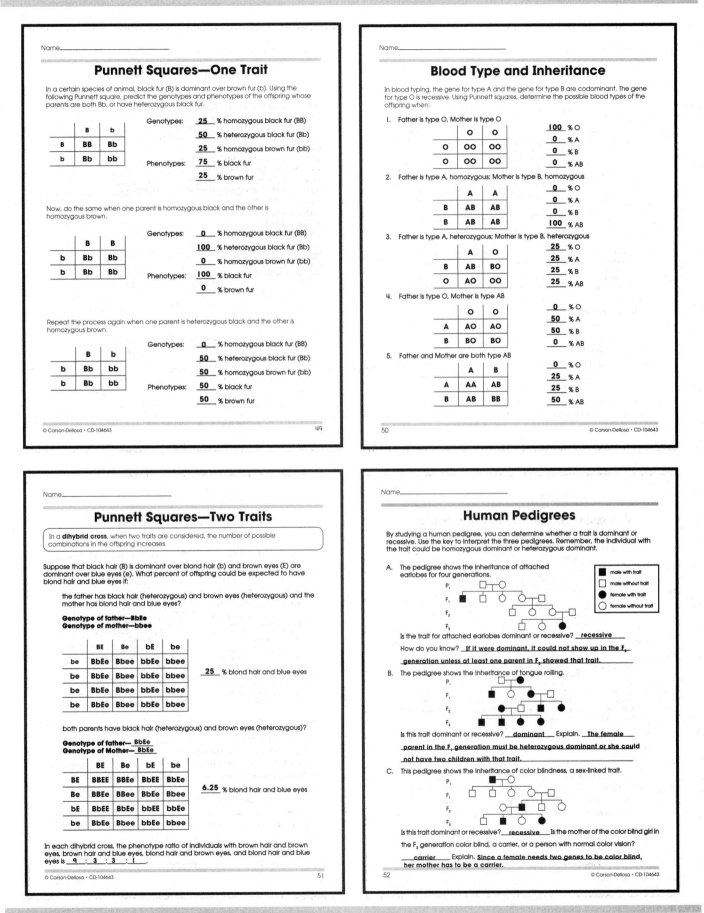

Punnett Squares—One Trait

Name_____

In a certain species of animal, black fur (B) is dominant over brown fur (b). Using the following Punnett square, predict the genotypes and phenotypes of the offspring whose parents are both Bb, or have heterozygous black fur.

	B	b
B	BB	Bb
b	Bb	bb

Genotypes:
__25__ % homozygous black fur (BB)
__50__ % heterozygous black fur (Bb)
__25__ % homozygous brown fur (bb)

Phenotypes:
__75__ % black fur
__25__ % brown fur

Now, do the same when one parent is homozygous black and the other is homozygous brown.

	B	B
b	Bb	Bb
b	Bb	Bb

Genotypes:
__0__ % homozygous black fur (BB)
__100__ % heterozygous black fur (Bb)
__0__ % homozygous brown fur (bb)

Phenotypes:
__100__ % black fur
__0__ % brown fur

Repeat the process again when one parent is heterozygous black and the other is homozygous brown.

	B	b
b	Bb	bb
b	Bb	bb

Genotypes:
__0__ % homozygous black fur (BB)
__50__ % heterozygous black fur (Bb)
__50__ % homozygous brown fur (bb)

Phenotypes:
__50__ % black fur
__50__ % brown fur

© Carson-Dellosa • CD-104643

49

Blood Type and Inheritance

Name_____

In blood typing, the gene for type A and the gene for type B are codominant. The gene for type O is recessive. Using Punnett squares, determine the possible blood types of the offspring when:

1. Father is type O, Mother is type O

	O	O
O	OO	OO
O	OO	OO

__100__ % O
__0__ % A
__0__ % B
__0__ % AB

2. Father is type A, homozygous; Mother is type B, homozygous

	A	A
B	AB	AB
B	AB	AB

__0__ % O
__0__ % A
__0__ % B
__100__ % AB

3. Father is type A, heterozygous; Mother is type B, heterozygous

	A	O
B	AB	BO
O	AO	OO

__25__ % O
__25__ % A
__25__ % B
__25__ % AB

4. Father is type O, Mother is type AB

	O	O
A	AO	AO
B	BO	BO

__0__ % O
__50__ % A
__50__ % B
__0__ % AB

5. Father and Mother are both type AB

	A	B
A	AA	AB
B	AB	BB

__0__ % O
__25__ % A
__25__ % B
__50__ % AB

50

© Carson-Dellosa • CD-104643

Punnett Squares—Two Traits

Name_____

In a **dihybrid cross**, when two traits are considered, the number of possible combinations in the offspring increases.

Suppose that black hair (B) is dominant over blond hair (b) and brown eyes (E) are dominant over blue eyes (e). What percent of offspring could be expected to have blond hair and blue eyes if:

the father has black hair (heterozygous) and brown eyes (heterozygous) and the mother has blond hair and blue eyes?

Genotype of father—BbEe
Genotype of mother—bbee

	BE	Be	bE	be
be	BbEe	Bbee	bbEe	bbee
be	BbEe	Bbee	bbEe	bbee
be	BbEe	Bbee	bbEe	bbee
be	BbEe	Bbee	bbEe	bbee

__25__ % blond hair and blue eyes

both parents have black hair (heterozygous) and brown eyes (heterozygous)?

Genotype of father— BbEe
Genotype of Mother— BbEe

	BE	Be	bE	be
BE	BBEE	BBEe	BbEE	BbEe
Be	BBEe	BBee	BbEe	Bbee
bE	BbEE	BbEe	bbEE	bbEe
be	BbEe	Bbee	bbEe	bbee

__6.25__ % blond hair and blue eyes

In each dihybrid cross, the phenotype ratio of individuals with brown hair and brown eyes, brown hair and blue eyes, blond hair and brown eyes, and blond hair and blue eyes is __9__ : __3__ : __3__ : __1__ .

© Carson-Dellosa • CD-104643

51

Human Pedigrees

Name_____

By studying a human pedigree, you can determine whether a trait is dominant or recessive. Use the key to interpret the three pedigrees. Remember, the individual with the trait could be homozygous dominant or heterozygous dominant.

A. The pedigree shows the inheritance of attached earlobes for four generations.

■	male with trait
☐	male without trait
●	female with trait
○	female without trait

P_1
F_1
F_2
F_3

Is the trait for attached earlobes dominant or recessive? __recessive__

How do you know? __If it were dominant, it could not show up in the F_2__ __generation unless at least one parent in F_1 showed that trait.__

B. The pedigree shows the inheritance of tongue rolling.

P_1
F_1
F_2
F_3

Is this trait dominant or recessive? __dominant__ Explain. __The female__ __parent in the F_1 generation must be heterozygous dominant or she could__ __not have two children with that trait.__

C. This pedigree shows the inheritance of color blindness, a sex-linked trait.

P_1
F_1
F_2
F_3

Is this trait dominant or recessive? __recessive__ Is the mother of the color blind girl in the F_3 generation color blind, a carrier, or a person with normal color vision?

__carrier__ Explain. __Since a female needs two genes to be color blind,__ __her mother has to be a carrier.__

52

© Carson-Dellosa • CD-104643

Answer Key

DNA Molecule and Replication

Name_____

The building blocks of the DNA molecule are **nucleotides**, which consist of a phosphate, a deoxyribose sugar, and a nitrogenous base.

The letters representing the four different nitrogeneous bases are shown in the nucleotides in the diagram. Place the name of the base next to its letter symbol.

A = ____adenine____

T = ____thymine____

G = ____guanine____

C = ____cytosine____

The DNA molecule has a double helix shape. Two strands of DNA are coiled around each other and attached by bonds between the nitrogenous bases of each chain. Adenine always bonds with thymine, and cytosine always bonds with guanine.

In the illustration, label a *phosphate* and a *deoxyribose sugar*. Fill in the symbol for each base depending on its complementary base in the opposite strand.

The second diagram shows the replication of DNA. Fill in the symbol for each base. Label the *original strand*, a *new strand*, and a *free-floating nucleotide*.

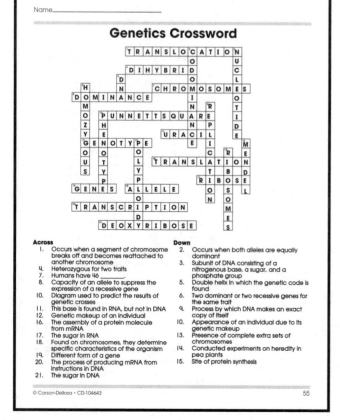

phosphate
original strand
sugar
free-floating nucleotides
new strand

Complete each sentence.

The credit for discovery of the structure of DNA was given to ____Watson____ and ____Crick____. The shape of the DNA molecule is described as a ____double helix____. After replication, ____two____ identical molecules of ____DNA____ are produced. A gene is a sequence of ____nucleotides____ in a DNA molecule.

---

mRNA and Transcription

Name_____

Transcription

Fill in the blanks. On the illustration of transcription, label the *DNA*, the *newly forming mRNA*, the *completed strand of mRNA*, and a *free nucleotide*.

Messenger RNA (mRNA) carries the instructions to make a particular ____protein____ of the DNA from the ____nucleus____ to the ribosomes. The process of producing mRNA from instructions in the DNA is called **transcription**. During transcription, the DNA molecule unwinds and separates, exposing the nitrogenous bases. Free RNA ____nucleotides____ pair with the exposed bases. No ____thymine____ (T) is in RNA. ____Uracil____ (U) pairs with adenine (A) instead. RNA contains the sugar ____ribase____ instead of deoxyribose. The mRNA molecule is completed by the formation of ____bonds____ between the RNA ____nucleotides____, and it then separates from the DNA. The mRNA molecule is a ____single____ strand, unlike DNA.

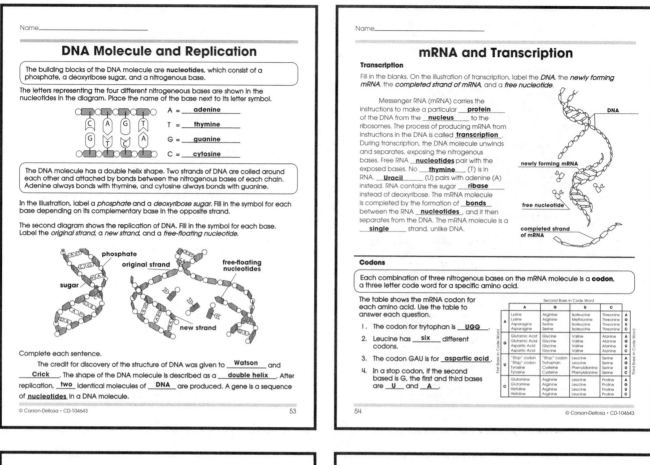

DNA
newly forming mRNA
free nucleotide
completed strand of mRNA

Codons

Each combination of three nitrogenous bases on the mRNA molecule is a **codon**, a three letter code word for a specific amino acid.

The table shows the mRNA codon for each amino acid. Use the table to answer each question.

1. The codon for trytophan is ____UGG____.

2. Leucine has ____six____ different codons.

3. The codon GAU is for ____aspartic acid____.

4. In a stop codon, if the second based is G, the first and third bases are ____U____ and ____A____.

First Base in Code Word	Second Base in Code Word A	G	U	C	Third Base in Code Word
A	Lysine / Lysine / Asparagine / Asparagine	Arginine / Arginine / Serine / Serine	Isoleucine / Methionine / Isoleucine / Isoleucine	Threonine / Threonine / Threonine / Threonine	A / G / U / C
G	Glutamic Acid / Glutamic Acid / Aspartic Acid / Aspartic Acid	Glycine / Glycine / Glycine / Glycine	Valine / Valine / Valine / Valine	Alanine / Alanine / Alanine / Alanine	A / G / U / C
U	"Stop" codon / "Stop" codon / Tyrosine / Tyrosine	"Stop" codon / Trytophan / Cysteine / Cysteine	Leucine / Leucine / Phenylalanine / Phenylalanine	Serine / Serine / Serine / Serine	A / G / U / C
C	Glutamine / Glutamine / Histidine / Histidine	Arginine / Arginine / Arginine / Arginine	Leucine / Leucine / Leucine / Leucine	Proline / Proline / Proline / Proline	A / G / U / C

Genetics Crossword

Name_____

Crossword answers:
- TRANSLOCATION
- DIHYBRID
- CHROMOSOMES
- DOMINANCE
- PUNNETTSQUARE
- URACIL
- GENOTYPE
- TRANSLATION
- RIBOSE
- GENES
- ALLELE
- TRANSCRIPTION
- DEOXYRIBOSE

Across
1. Occurs when a segment of chromosome breaks off and becomes reattached to another chromosome
4. Heterozygous for two traits
7. Humans have 46 _____.
8. Capacity of an allele to suppress the expression of a recessive gene
10. Diagram used to predict the results of genetic crosses
11. This base is found in RNA, but not in DNA
12. Genetic makeup of an individual
16. The assembly of a protein molecule from mRNA
17. The sugar in RNA
18. Found on chromosomes, they determine specific characteristics of the organism
19. Different form of a gene
20. The process of producing mRNA from instructions in the DNA
21. The sugar in DNA

Down
2. Occurs when both alleles are equally dominant
3. Subunit of DNA consisting of a nitrogenous base, a sugar, and a phosphate group
5. Double helix in which the genetic code is found
6. Two dominant or two recessive genes for the same trait
9. Process by which DNA makes an exact copy of itself
10. Appearance of an individual due to its genetic makeup
13. Presence of complete extra sets of chromosomes
14. Conducted experiments on heredity in pea plants
15. Site of protein synthesis

Life Activities and Body Systems

Name_____

Match each life activity with its example.

1. nutrition ____c____
2. circulation ____e____
3. respiration ____b____
4. excretion ____f____
5. synthesis ____d____
6. regulation ____h____
7. growth ____k____
8. reproduction ____a____
9. metabolism ____j____
10. homeostasis ____g____
11. digestion ____i____

a. a cat has a litter of six kittens
b. the cells utilize glucose to produce energy
c. a plant absorbs minerals from the soil
d. a plant forms large starch molecules from smaller sugar molecules
e. the bloodstream brings oxygen and food to the cells
f. waste products are eliminated during perspiration
g. a person sweats to keep body temperature at a safe level
h. the brain coordinates the various systems of the body
i. process by which food is changed into a form the body can use
j. the human body produces hormones, vitamins, proteins, enzymes, etc. to keep it functioning
k. a 7-pound baby becomes a 180-pound man

Complete each sentence.

The lungs are the main organ of the ____respiratory____ system, but they are also an organ in the ____excretory____ system. The lymph and the lymphatics are part of the ____circulatory____ system. Although food does not pass through the liver and gallbladder, they are part of the ____digestive____ system. As a duct gland, the pancreas is part of the ____digestive____ system. As a ductless gland, the pancreas is part of the ____endocrine____ system. The hypothalamus, through its neurosecretory cells, coordinates the activities of the ____endocrine____ and ____nervous____ systems.

Answer Key

Life Activities Crossword

Name_____

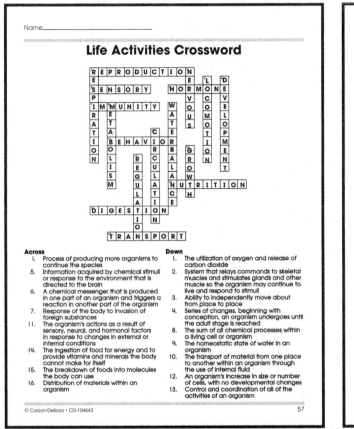

Across

1. Process of producing more organisms to continue the species
5. Information acquired by chemical stimuli or response to the environment that is directed to the brain
6. A chemical messenger that is produced in one part of an organism and triggers a reaction in another part of the organism
7. Response of the body to invasion of foreign substances
11. The organism's actions as a result of sensory, neural, and hormonal factors in response to changes in external or internal conditions
14. The ingestion of food for energy and to provide vitamins and minerals the body cannot make for itself
15. The breakdown of foods into molecules the body can use
16. Distribution of materials within an organism

Down

1. The utilization of oxygen and release of carbon dioxide
2. System that relays commands to skeletal muscles and stimulates glands and other muscle so the organism may continue to live and respond to stimuli
3. Ability to independently move about from place to place
4. Series of changes, beginning with conception, an organism undergoes until the adult stage is reached
8. The sum of all chemical processes within a living cell or organism
9. The homeostatic state of water in an organism
10. The transport of material from one place to another within an organism through the use of internal fluid
12. An organism's increase in size or number of cells, with no developmental changes
13. Control and coordination of all of the activities of an organism

---

The Frog

Name_____

Digestive System
Label the parts of a frog's digestive system.

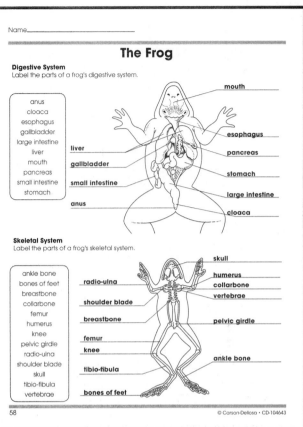

anus
cloaca
esophagus
gallbladder
large intestine
liver
mouth
pancreas
small intestine
stomach

mouth
esophagus
pancreas
stomach
large intestine
cloaca
liver
gallbladder
small intestine
anus

Skeletal System
Label the parts of a frog's skeletal system.

ankle bone
bones of feet
breastbone
collarbone
femur
humerus
knee
pelvic girdle
radio-ulna
shoulder blade
skull
tibio-fibula
vertebrae

radio-ulna
shoulder blade
breastbone
femur
knee
tibio-fibula
bones of feet

skull
humerus
collarbone
vertebrae
pelvic girdle
ankle bone

The Frog

Name_____

Nervous System
Label the parts of a frog's nervous system.

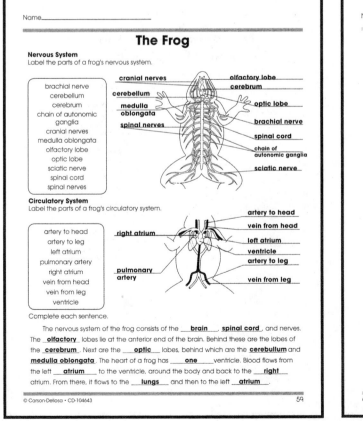

brachial nerve
cerebellum
cerebrum
chain of autonomic ganglia
cranial nerves
medulla oblongata
olfactory lobe
optic lobe
sciatic nerve
spinal cord
spinal nerves

cranial nerves
cerebellum
medulla oblongata
spinal nerves

olfactory lobe
cerebrum
optic lobe
brachial nerve
spinal cord
chain of autonomic ganglia
sciatic nerve

Circulatory System
Label the parts of a frog's circulatory system.

artery to head
artery to leg
left atrium
pulmonary artery
right atrium
vein from head
vein from leg
ventricle

right atrium
pulmonary artery

artery to head
vein from head
left atrium
ventricle
artery to leg
vein from leg

Complete each sentence.

The nervous system of the frog consists of the __**brain**__ , __**spinal cord**__ , and nerves. The __**olfactory**__ lobes lie at the anterior end of the brain. Behind these are the lobes of the __**cerebrum**__. Next are the __**optic**__ lobes, behind which are the __**cerebellum**__ and __**medulla oblongata**__. The heart of a frog has __**one**__ ventricle. Blood flows from the left __**atrium**__ to the ventricle, around the body and back to the __**right**__ atrium. From there, it flows to the __**lungs**__ and then to the left __**atrium**__ .

The Frog

Name_____

Urinary System
Label the parts of a female frog's urinary system.

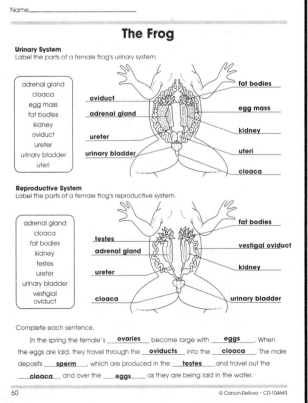

adrenal gland
cloaca
egg mass
fat bodies
kidney
oviduct
ureter
urinary bladder
uteri

oviduct
adrenal gland
ureter
urinary bladder

fat bodies
egg mass
kidney
uteri
cloaca

Reproductive System
Label the parts of a female frog's reproductive system.

adrenal gland
cloaca
fat bodies
kidney
testes
ureter
urinary bladder
vestigial oviduct

testes
adrenal gland
ureter
cloaca

fat bodies
vestigial oviduct
kidney
urinary bladder

Complete each sentence.

In the spring the female's __**ovaries**__ become large with __**eggs**__ . When the eggs are laid, they travel through the __**oviducts**__ into the __**cloaca**__ . The male deposits __**sperm**__ , which are produced in the __**testes**__ and travel out the __**cloaca**__ and over the __**eggs**__ as they are being laid in the water.

Answer Key

The Earthworm

Digestive System
Label the parts of an earthworm's digestive system.

anus
crop
esophagus
gizzard
intestine
mouth

intestine

crop

anus

mouth   esophagus   gizzard

Reproductive System
Label the parts of an earthworm's reproductive system.

clitellum
ovary
sperm
receptacle
sperm resevoir
testis

clitellum

testis

sperm resevoir

ovary   sperm receptacle

Complete each sentence.

After food enters the mouth, it passes through the **esophagus** and is then stored in the **crop**. From there, it passes to the **gizzard**, where it is mechanically broken down by grinding. After this, it is chemically broken down in the **intestine**. Undigested material is egested through the **anus**. Since an earthworm produces both eggs and sperm, it is considered to be a **hermaphrodite**. However, an earthworm **cannot** self-fertilize.

© Carson-Dellosa • CD-104643   61

The Grasshopper

External Anatomy
Label the parts of a grasshopper's external anatomy. **Use brackets to indicate the three regions of the body: head, thorax, and abdomen.**

antenna
compound eye
ear
egg-laying apparatus
legs
simple eye
spiracles
wings

thorax
antenna
head   wings
abdomen
simple eye
compound eye
legs   egg-laying apparatus
ear   spiracles

Digestive System
Label the parts of a grasshopper's digestive system.

anus
crop
gastric caeca
gizzard
intestine
mouth
rectum
salivary glands
stomach

gizzard
crop   rectum
anus
mouth
intestine
gastric caeca   stomach

Complete each sentence.

The grasshopper ingests food through the **mouth**. The food is temporarily stored in the **crop**, after which it passes to the **gizzard** for mechanical grinding. Digestion takes place in the **stomach** and **intestine**. Undigested waste is egested through the **anus**. On its thorax, a grasshopper has **three** pairs of **jointed** legs and **two** pairs of wings. The **spiracles** on the abdomen are used to carry oxygen.

62   © Carson-Dellosa • CD-104643

Circulatory Systems of the Earthworm and Grasshopper

Label the parts of an earthworm's circulatory system.

aortic arches
dorsal blood vessel
ventral blood vessel

dorsal blood vessel

aortic arches

ventral blood vessel

Label the parts of a grasshopper's circulatory system.

aorta
heart
sinuses

aorta

heart

sinuses

Complete each sentence.

1. Which organism has an open circulatory system? **grasshopper**
2. Which organism has a closed circulatory system? **earthworm**
3. Which type of blood vessel is the aorta? **artery**
4. In the earthworm, the aortic arches act as **hearts**.
5. In the earthworm, blood flows from the **dorsal** blood vessel to the **ventral** blood vessel.
6. In a grasshopper, blood re-enters the heart through several pairs of ostia, or **pores**.

© Carson-Dellosa • CD-104643   63

Nervous Systems of the Earthworm and Grasshopper

Label the parts of an earthworm's nervous system.

brain
ganglia
nerves
ventral nerve cord

nerves

brain

ventral nerve cord

ganglia

Label the parts of a grasshopper's nervous system.

antennae
brain
compound eye
ganglia
nerves
ventral nerve cord

antennae

compound eye

brain

ventral nerve cord
ganglia

nerves

Complete each sentence.

In the earthworm, two nerves from the paired **brain** run around each side of the **pharynx** to the **ventral** side of the worm. Here they join to become a double **nerve** cord that runs to the last segment. In each **segment**, they join to become an enlarged **ganglian**.

In the grasshopper, the most prominent parts of the brain are the **optic** lobes. The large **compound** eyes are made up of many **lenses** so the grasshopper can see in many directions at the same time. The **ventral** nerve cord contains many **ganglia**. The largest ganglion sends messages to the **jumping** legs.

64   © Carson-Dellosa • CD-104643

Answer Key

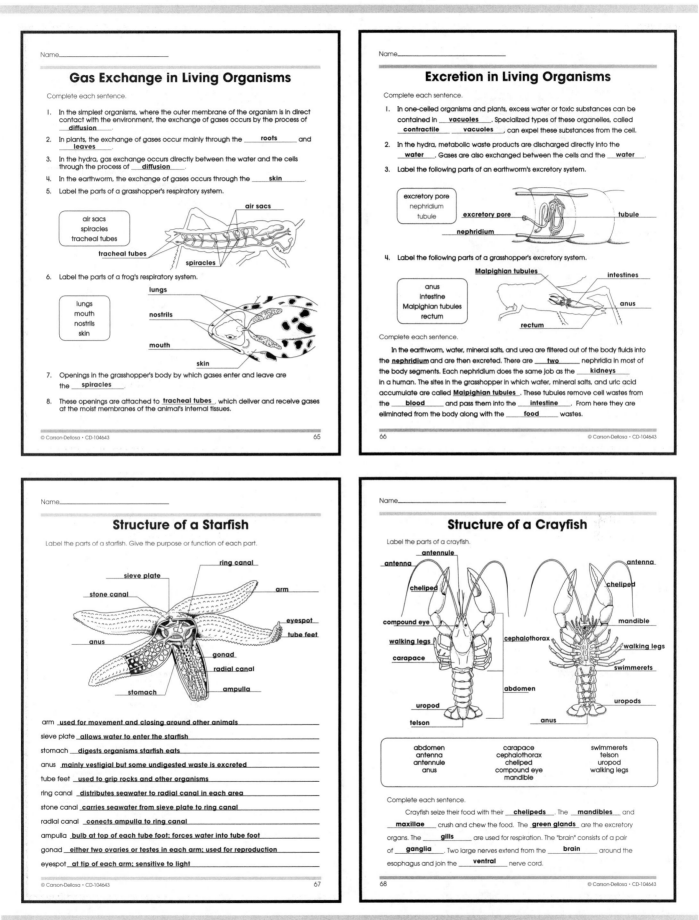

Gas Exchange in Living Organisms

Complete each sentence.

1. In the simplest organisms, where the outer membrane of the organism is in direct contact with the environment, the exchange of gases occurs by the process of __diffusion__.

2. In plants, the exchange of gases occur mainly through the __roots__ and __leaves__.

3. In the hydra, gas exchange occurs directly between the water and the cells through the process of __diffusion__.

4. In the earthworm, the exchange of gases occurs through the __skin__.

5. Label the parts of a grasshopper's respiratory system.

   air sacs
   spiracles
   tracheal tubes

   air sacs
   tracheal tubes
   spiracles

6. Label the parts of a frog's respiratory system.

   lungs
   mouth
   nostrils
   skin

   lungs
   nostrils
   mouth
   skin

7. Openings in the grasshopper's body by which gases enter and leave are the __spiracles__.

8. These openings are attached to __tracheal tubes__, which deliver and receive gases at the moist membranes of the animal's internal tissues.

Excretion in Living Organisms

Complete each sentence.

1. In one-celled organisms and plants, excess water or toxic substances can be contained in __vacuoles__. Specialized types of these organelles, called __contractile__ __vacuoles__, can expel these substances from the cell.

2. In the hydra, metabolic waste products are discharged directly into the __water__. Gases are also exchanged between the cells and the __water__.

3. Label the following parts of an earthworm's excretory system.

   excretory pore
   nephridium
   tubule

   excretory pore
   nephridium
   tubule

4. Label the following parts of a grasshopper's excretory system.

   anus
   intestine
   Malpighian tubules
   rectum

   Malpighian tubules
   intestines
   anus
   rectum

Complete each sentence.

In the earthworm, water, mineral salts, and urea are filtered out of the body fluids into the __nephridium__ and are then excreted. There are __two__ nephridia in most of the body segments. Each nephridium does the same job as the __kidneys__ in a human. The sites in the grasshopper in which water, mineral salts, and uric acid accumulate are called __Malpighian tubules__. These tubules remove cell wastes from the __blood__ and pass them into the __intestine__. From here they are eliminated from the body along with the __food__ wastes.

Structure of a Starfish

Label the parts of a starfish. Give the purpose or function of each part.

ring canal
sieve plate
stone canal
arm
eyespot
tube feet
anus
gonad
radial canal
ampulla
stomach

arm __used for movement and closing around other animals__

sieve plate __allows water to enter the starfish__

stomach __digests organisms starfish eats__

anus __mainly vestigial but some undigested waste is excreted__

tube feet __used to grip rocks and other organisms__

ring canal __distributes seawater to radial canal in each area__

stone canal __carries seawater from sieve plate to ring canal__

radial canal __conects ampulla to ring canal__

ampulla __bulb at top of each tube foot; forces water into tube foot__

gonad __either two ovaries or testes in each arm; used for reproduction__

eyespot __at tip of each arm; sensitive to light__

Structure of a Crayfish

Label the parts of a crayfish.

antennule
antenna
cheliped
compound eye
walking legs
carapace
uropod
telson

antenna
cheliped
mandible
walking legs
swimmerets
uropods
anus

cephalothorax
abdomen

abdomen	carapace	swimmerets
antenna	cephalothorax	telson
antennule	cheliped	uropod
anus	compound eye	walking legs
	mandible	

Complete each sentence.

Crayfish seize their food with their __chelipeds__. The __mandibles__ and __maxillae__ crush and chew the food. The __green glands__ are the excretory organs. The __gills__ are used for respiration. The "brain" consists of a pair of __ganglia__. Two large nerves extend from the __brain__ around the esophagus and join the __ventral__ nerve cord.

Answer Key

Structure of a Bony Fish

Label the parts of a fish.

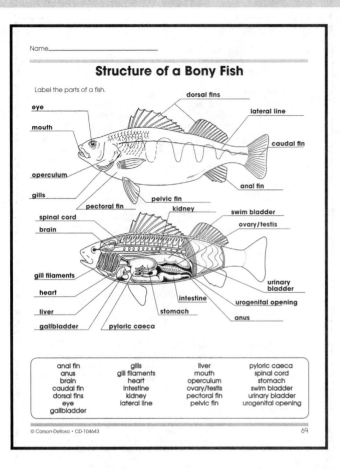

- eye
- mouth
- dorsal fins
- lateral line
- caudal fin
- operculum
- gills
- anal fin
- pectoral fin
- pelvic fin
- kidney
- swim bladder
- spinal cord
- ovary/testis
- brain
- gill filaments
- heart
- liver
- gallbladder
- pyloric caeca
- intestine
- stomach
- urinary bladder
- urogenital opening
- anus

anal fin	gills	liver	pyloric caeca
anus	gill filaments	mouth	spinal cord
brain	heart	operculum	stomach
caudal fin	intestine	ovary/testis	swim bladder
dorsal fins	kidney	pectoral fin	urinary bladder
eye	lateral line	pelvic fin	urogenital opening
gallbladder			

69

Internal Structure of a Bird

Label the parts of a bird's internal structure.

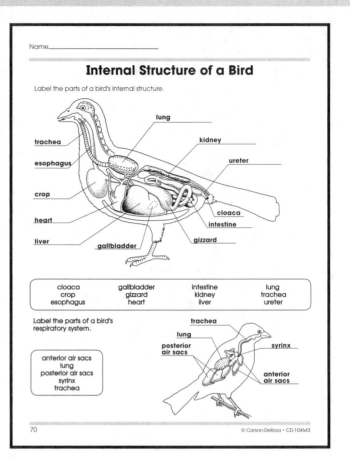

- trachea
- esophagus
- crop
- heart
- liver
- lung
- kidney
- ureter
- cloaca
- intestine
- gizzard
- gallbladder

cloaca	gallbladder	intestine	lung
crop	gizzard	kidney	trachea
esophagus	heart	liver	ureter

Label the parts of a bird's respiratory system.

| anterior air sacs |
| lung |
| posterior air sacs |
| syrinx |
| trachea |

- trachea
- lung
- posterior air sacs
- syrinx
- anterior air sacs

70

The Human Skeletal System

Label the parts of a human's skeletal system. Then, label each of the four types of movable joints.

| carpals |
| clavicle |
| cranium |
| femur |
| fibula |
| humerus |
| mandible |
| metacarpals |
| metatarsals |
| patella |
| pectoral girdle |
| pelvic girdle |
| phalanges |
| radius |
| ribs |
| scapula |
| skull |
| sternum |
| tarsals |
| tibia |
| ulna |
| vertebrae |
| vertebral column |

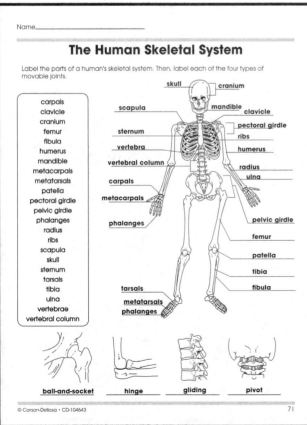

- skull
- cranium
- scapula
- mandible
- clavicle
- sternum
- pectoral girdle
- ribs
- vertebra
- humerus
- vertebral column
- radius
- carpals
- ulna
- metacarpals
- phalanges
- pelvic girdle
- femur
- patella
- tibia
- fibula
- tarsals
- metatarsals
- phalanges

- ball-and-socket
- hinge
- gliding
- pivot

71

Structure of Bones

Label the parts of a long bone on both diagrams. The diagram at the right shows a longitudinal section; the other, a cross section.

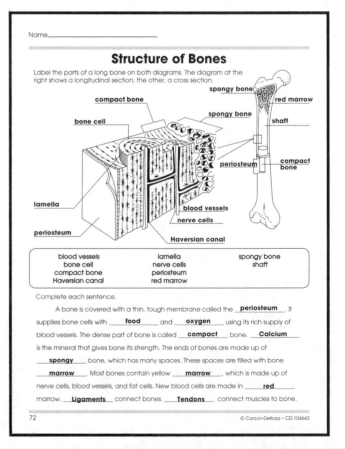

- compact bone
- bone cell
- lamella
- periosteum
- spongy bone
- spongy bone
- blood vessels
- nerve cells
- Haversian canal
- spongy bone
- red marrow
- shaft
- periosteum
- compact bone

blood vessels	lamella	spongy bone
bone cell	nerve cells	shaft
compact bone	periosteum	
Haversian canal	red marrow	

Complete each sentence.

A bone is covered with a thin, tough membrane called the __periosteum__. It supplies bone cells with __food__ and __oxygen__ using its rich supply of blood vessels. The dense part of bone is called __compact__ bone. __Calcium__ is the mineral that gives bone its strength. The ends of bones are made up of __spongy__ bone, which has many spaces. These spaces are filled with bone __marrow__. Most bones contain yellow __marrow__, which is made up of nerve cells, blood vessels, and fat cells. New blood cells are made in __red__ marrow. __Ligaments__ connect bones. __Tendons__ connect muscles to bone.

72

Answer Key

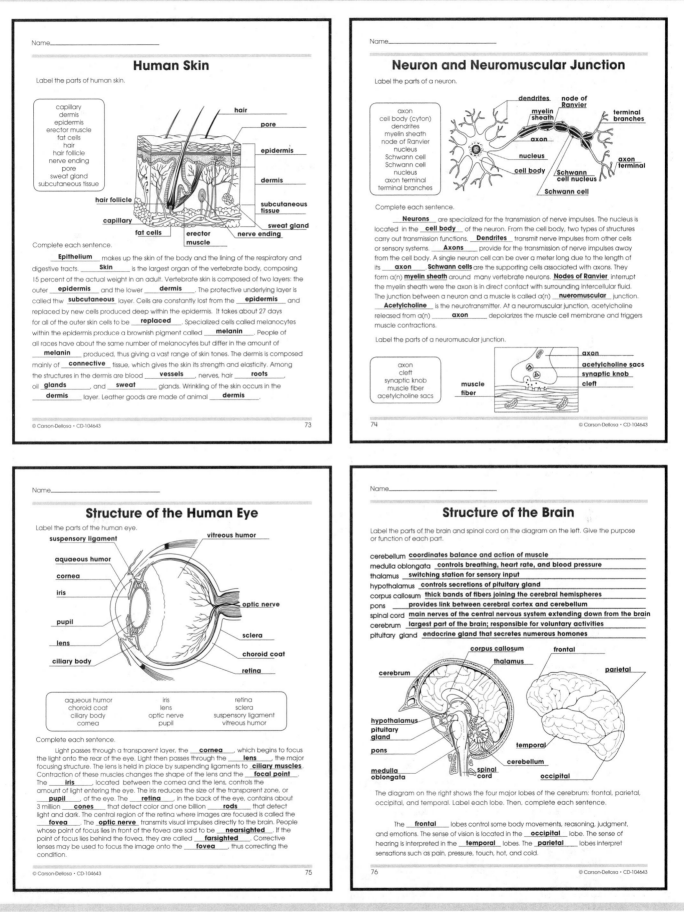

Human Skin

Name_____

Human Skin

Label the parts of human skin.

capillary
dermis
epidermis
erector muscle
fat cells
hair
hair follicle
nerve ending
pore
sweat gland
subcutaneous tissue

hair
pore
epidermis
dermis
subcutaneous tissue
sweat gland
nerve ending
erector muscle
fat cells
capillary
hair follicle

Complete each sentence.

__Epithelium__ makes up the skin of the body and the lining of the respiratory and digestive tracts. __Skin__ is the largest organ of the vertebrate body, composing 15 percent of the actual weight in an adult. Vertebrate skin is composed of two layers: the outer __epidermis__ and the lower __dermis__. The protective underlying layer is called thw __subcutaneous__ layer. Cells are constantly lost from the __epidermis__ and replaced by new cells produced deep within the epidermis. It takes about 27 days for all of the outer skin cells to be __replaced__. Specialized cells called melanocytes within the epidermis produce a brownish pigment called __melanin__. People of all races have about the same number of melanocytes but differ in the amount of __melanin__ produced, thus giving a vast range of skin tones. The dermis is composed mainly of __connective__ tissue, which gives the skin its strength and elasticity. Among the structures in the dermis are blood __vessels__, nerves, hair __roots__, oil __glands__, and __sweat__ glands. Wrinkling of the skin occurs in the __dermis__ layer. Leather goods are made of animal __dermis__.

© Carson-Dellosa • CD-104643   73

Name_____

Neuron and Neuromuscular Junction

Label the parts of a neuron.

axon
cell body (cyton)
dendrites
myelin sheath
node of Ranvier
nucleus
Schwann cell
Schwann cell nucleus
axon terminal
terminal branches

dendrites
node of Ranvier
myelin sheath
terminal branches
axon
nucleus
axon terminal
cell body
Schwann cell nucleus
Schwann cell

Complete each sentence.

__Neurons__ are specialized for the transmission of nerve impulses. The nucleus is located in the __cell body__ of the neuron. From the cell body, two types of structures carry out transmission functions. __Dendrites__ transmit nerve impulses from other cells or sensory systems. __Axons__ provide for the transmission of nerve impulses away from the cell body. A single neuron cell can be over a meter long due to the length of its __axon__. Schwann cells are the supporting cells associated with axons. They form a(n) __myelin sheath__ around many vertebrate neurons. __Nodes of Ranvier__ interrupt the myelin sheath were the axon is in direct contact with surrounding intercellular fluid. The junction between a neuron and a muscle is called a(n) __nueromuscular__ junction. __Acetylcholine__ is the neurotransmitter. At a neuromuscular junction, acetylcholine released from a(n) __axon__ depolarizes the muscle cell membrane and triggers muscle contractions.

Label the parts of a neuromuscular junction.

axon
cleft
synaptic knob
muscle fiber
acetylcholine sacs

muscle fiber

axon
acetylcholine sacs
synaptic knob
cleft

74   © Carson-Dellosa • CD-104643

Name_____

Structure of the Human Eye

Label the parts of the human eye.

suspensory ligament
aquaeous humor
cornea
iris
pupil
lens
ciliary body

vitreous humor
optic nerve
sclera
choroid coat
retina

aqueous humor
choroid coat
ciliary body
cornea
iris
lens
optic nerve
pupil
retina
sclera
suspensory ligament
vitreous humor

Complete each sentence.

Light passes through a transparent layer, the __cornea__, which begins to focus the light onto the rear of the eye. Light then passes through the __lens__, the major focusing structure. The lens is held in place by suspending ligaments to __ciliary muscles__. Contraction of these muscles changes the shape of the lens and the __focal point__. The __iris__, located between the cornea and the lens, controls the amount of light entering the eye. The __retina__, in the back of the eye, contains about 3 million __cones__ that detect color and one billion __rods__ that detect light and dark. The central region of the retina where images are focused is called the __fovea__. The __optic nerve__ transmits visual impulses directly to the brain. People whose point of focus lies in front of the fovea are said to be __nearsighted__. If the point of focus lies behind the fovea, they are called __farsighted__. Corrective lenses may be used to focus the image onto the __fovea__, thus correcting the condition.

© Carson-Dellosa • CD-104643   75

Name_____

Structure of the Brain

Label the parts of the brain and spinal cord on the diagram on the left. Give the purpose or function of each part.

cerebellum __coordinates balance and action of muscle__
medulla oblongata __controls breathing, heart rate, and blood pressure__
thalamus __switching station for sensory input__
hypothalamus __controls secretions of pituitary gland__
corpus callosum __thick bands of fibers joining the cerebral hemispheres__
pons __provides link between cerebral cortex and cerebellum__
spinal cord __main nerves of the central nervous system extending down from the brain__
cerebrum __largest part of the brain; responsible for voluntary activities__
pituitary gland __endocrine gland that secretes numerous homones__

corpus callosum
thalamus
frontal
cerebrum
parietal
hypothalamus
pituitary gland
temporal
pons
cerebellum
occipital
medulla oblongata
spinal cord

The diagram on the right shows the four major lobes of the cerebrum: frontal, parietal, occipital, and temporal. Label each lobe. Then, complete each sentence.

The __frontal__ lobes control some body movements, reasoning, judgment, and emotions. The sense of vision is located in the __occipital__ lobe. The sense of hearing is interpreted in the __temporal__ lobes. The __parietal__ lobes interpret sensations such as pain, pressure, touch, hot, and cold.

76   © Carson-Dellosa • CD-104643

Answer Key

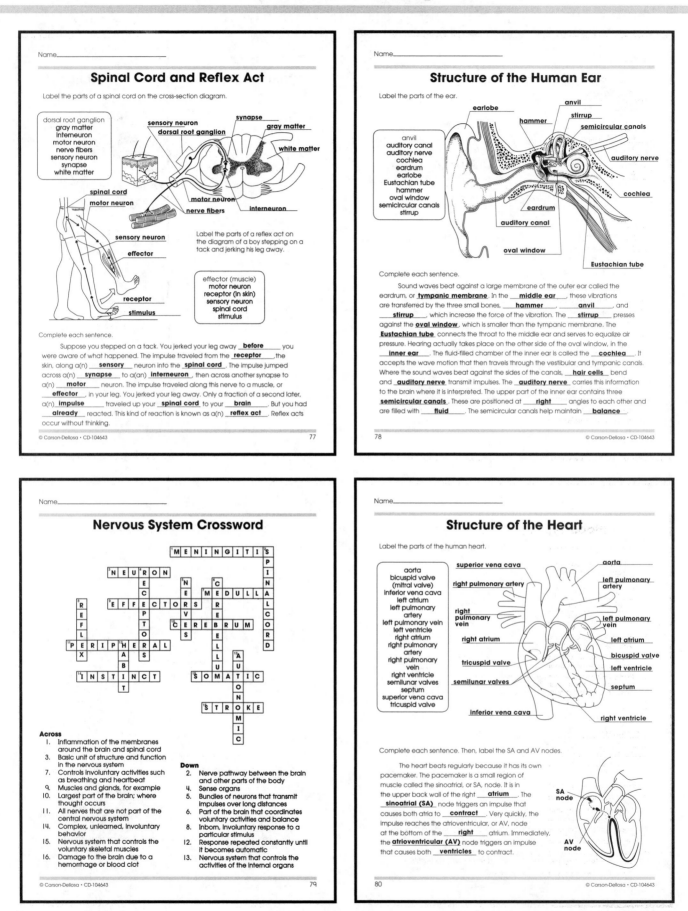

Spinal Cord and Reflex Act

Label the parts of a spinal cord on the cross-section diagram.

dorsal root ganglion
gray matter
interneuron
motor neuron
nerve fibers
sensory neuron
synapse
white matter

sensory neuron
dorsal root ganglion
synapse
gray matter
white matter

spinal cord
motor neuron
motor neuron
nerve fibers
interneuron

sensory neuron
effector
receptor
stimulus

Label the parts of a reflex act on the diagram of a boy stepping on a tack and jerking his leg away.

effector (muscle)
motor neuron
receptor (in skin)
sensory neuron
spinal cord
stimulus

Complete each sentence.

Suppose you stepped on a tack. You jerked your leg away **before** you were aware of what happened. The impulse traveled from the **receptor**, the skin, along a(n) **sensory** neuron into the **spinal cord**. The impulse jumped across a(n) **synapse** to a(an) **interneuron**, then across another synapse to a(n) **motor** neuron. The impulse traveled along this nerve to a muscle, or **effector**, in your leg. You jerked your leg away. Only a fraction of a second later, a(n) **impulse** traveled up your **spinal cord** to your **brain**. But you had **already** reacted. This kind of reaction is known as a(n) **reflex act**. Reflex acts occur without thinking.

© Carson-Dellosa • CD-104643

77

Structure of the Human Ear

Label the parts of the ear.

anvil
auditory canal
auditory nerve
cochlea
eardrum
earlobe
Eustachian tube
hammer
oval window
semicircular canals
stirrup

earlobe
hammer
anvil
stirrup
semicircular canals
auditory nerve
cochlea
eardrum
auditory canal
oval window
Eustachian tube

Complete each sentence.

Sound waves beat against a large membrane of the outer ear called the eardrum, or **tympanic membrane**. In the **middle ear**, these vibrations are transferred by the three small bones, **hammer**, **anvil**, and **stirrup**, which increase the force of the vibration. The **stirrup** presses against the **oval window**, which is smaller than the tympanic membrane. The **Eustachian tube** connects the throat to the middle ear and serves to equalize air pressure. Hearing actually takes place on the other side of the oval window, in the **inner ear**. The fluid-filled chamber of the inner ear is called the **cochlea**. It accepts the wave motion that then travels through the vestibular and tympanic canals. Where the sound waves beat against the sides of the canals, **hair cells** bend and **auditory nerve** transmit impulses. The **auditory nerve** carries this information to the brain where it is interpreted. The upper part of the inner ear contains three **semicircular canals**. These are positioned at **right** angles to each other and are filled with **fluid**. The semicircular canals help maintain **balance**.

78

© Carson-Dellosa • CD-104643

Nervous System Crossword

M E N I N G I T I S
N E U R O N
E F F E C T O R S
M E D U L L A
C E R E B R U M
P E R I P H E R A L
I N S T I N C T
S O M A T I C
S T R O K E

Across
1. Inflammation of the membranes around the brain and spinal cord
3. Basic unit of structure and function in the nervous system
7. Controls involuntary activities such as breathing and heartbeat
9. Muscles and glands, for example
10. Largest part of the brain; where thought occurs
11. All nerves that are not part of the central nervous system
14. Complex, unlearned, involuntary behavior
15. Nervous system that controls the voluntary skeletal muscles
16. Damage to the brain due to a hemorrhage or blood clot

Down
2. Nerve pathway between the brain and other parts of the body
4. Sense organs
5. Bundles of neurons that transmit impulses over long distances
6. Part of the brain that coordinates voluntary activities and balance
8. Inborn, involuntary response to a particular stimulus
12. Response repeated constantly until it becomes automatic
13. Nervous system that controls the activities of the internal organs

© Carson-Dellosa • CD-104643

79

Structure of the Heart

Label the parts of the human heart.

aorta
bicuspid valve
(mitral valve)
inferior vena cava
left atrium
left pulmonary artery
left pulmonary vein
left ventricle
right atrium
right pulmonary artery
right pulmonary vein
right ventricle
semilunar valves
septum
superior vena cava
tricuspid valve

superior vena cava
right pulmonary artery
right pulmonary vein
right atrium
tricuspid valve
semilunar valves
inferior vena cava
aorta
left pulmonary artery
left pulmonary vein
left atrium
bicuspid valve
left ventricle
septum
right ventricle

Complete each sentence. Then, label the SA and AV nodes.

The heart beats regularly because it has its own pacemaker. The pacemaker is a small region of muscle called the sinoatrial, or SA, node. It is in the upper back wall of the right **atrium**. The **sinoatrial (SA)** node triggers an impulse that causes both atria to **contract**. Very quickly, the impulse reaches the atrioventricular, or AV, node at the bottom of the **right** atrium. Immediately, the **atrioventricular (AV)** node triggers an impulse that causes both **ventricles** to contract.

SA node

AV node

80

© Carson-Dellosa • CD-104643

Answer Key

Name_____

The Human Circulatory System

Starting from and ending with the right atrium, trace the flow of blood through the heart and body by numbering each stage in the correct order.

1, 11	right atrium	**4**	lungs
6	left atrium	**2**	right ventricle
3	pulmonary artery	**7**	left ventricle
10	vena cava	**9**	body cells
8	aorta	**5**	pulmonary veins

Starting from and ending with the heart, trace the flow of blood through the human circulatory system and body by numbering each stage in the correct order.

1, 7	heart	**4**	capillaries
6	veins	**2**	arteries
3	arterioles	**5**	venules

Write the term that best fits each description.

1.	vessels that carry blood away from the heart	**arteries**
2.	vessels that carry blood toward the heart	**veins**
3.	tiny blood vessels with walls that are only one cell thick	**capillaries**
4.	thick wall that divides the heart into two sides	**septum**
5.	upper chambers of the heart that receive blood	**atria**
6.	lower chambers of the heart that pump blood out of the heart	**ventricles**
7.	valve between right atrium and right ventricle	**tricuspid**
8.	valve between left atrium and left ventricle	**mitral (bicuspid)**
9.	valves found between the ventricles and blood vessels	**semilunar**
10.	membrane around the heart	**pericardium**
11.	the only artery in the body rich in carbon dioxide	**pulmonary artery**
12.	the only vein in the body rich in oxygen	**pulmonary vein**

81

Name_____

The Blood

Label the parts on the diagram. Then, answer each question.

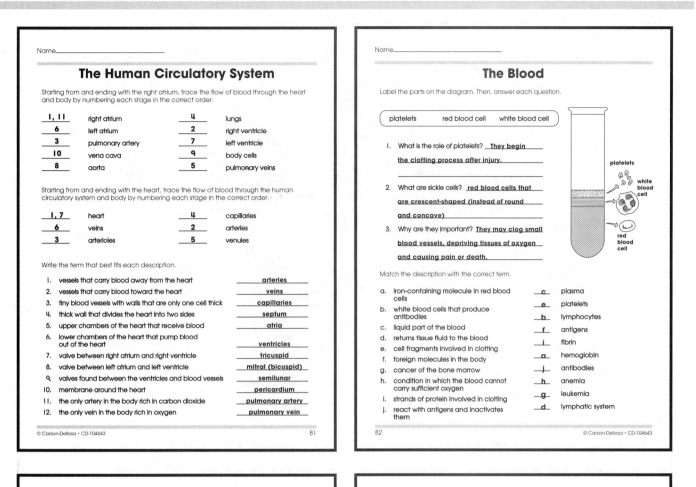

platelets   red blood cell   white blood cell

1. What is the role of platelets? **They begin the clotting process after injury.**

2. What are sickle cells? **red blood cells that are crescent-shaped (instead of round and concave)**

3. Why are they important? **They may clog small blood vessels, depriving tissues of oxygen and causing pain or death.**

Match the description with the correct term.

a.	iron-containing molecule in red blood cells	**c**	plasma
b.	white blood cells that produce antibodies	**e**	platelets
c.	liquid part of the blood	**b**	lymphocytes
d.	returns tissue fluid to the blood	**f**	antigens
e.	cell fragments involved in clotting	**i**	fibrin
f.	foreign molecules in the body	**a**	hemoglobin
g.	cancer of the bone marrow	**j**	antibodies
h.	condition in which the blood cannot carry sufficient oxygen	**h**	anemia
i.	strands of protein involved in clotting	**g**	leukemia
j.	react with antigens and inactivates them	**d**	lymphatic system

82

Name_____

Blood Types and Transfusions

Complete the table. Then, answer each question.

Blood Type	Antigens on Red Cells	Antibodies in Plasma	May Donate To	May Receive From
A	A	anti-B	A, AB	A
B	B	anti-A	B, AB	B, O
AB	A, B	none	AB	A, B, AB, O
O	none	anti-A, anti-B	A, B, AB, O	O

1. Why are individuals with blood type O considered universal donors? **People any type can recieve blood from type O.**

2. Why are individuals with blood type AB considered universal recipients? **They can receive any type of blood.**

3. Today, some people who know they must undergo surgery in the near future give their own blood at the blood bank. Then, they use it during surgery. Why?
   They can guarantee there are no issues with compatibilty or diseases.

The distribution of blood types around the world varies. For example, it is different in Japan and among Basque people in northern Spain.

POPULATION	A	B	AB	O
Australia	38%	10%	3%	49%
Philippines	23%	25%	6%	46%
Canada	42%	9%	3%	46%

Blood typing information taken from Australian Red Cross, Red Cross of the Philippines, and Canadian Blood Services.

Use the table to answer each question.

1. In Canada, what is the most common blood type? **O**

2. If you were Australian, what are the chances that your blood type is A? **38%**

3. What country has the lowest representation of type A? **Philippines**

4. What blood type is least common in all three countries? **AB**

5. Compare the frequency of type B blood between Australians and Canadians. **A similar percentage has type B in each country, but Australians are slightly more likely to be type B.**

83

Name_____

The Human Digestive System

Label the parts of the human digestive system.

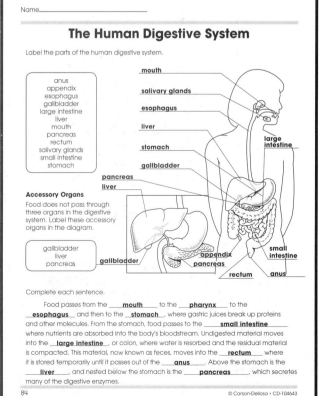

anus
appendix
esophagus
gallbladder
large intestine
liver
mouth
pancreas
rectum
salivary glands
small intestine
stomach

mouth
salivary glands
esophagus
liver
stomach
gallbladder
pancreas
liver
large intestine
small intestine
rectum
anus

Accessory Organs

Food does not pass through three organs in the digestive system. Label these accessory organs in the diagram.

gallbladder
liver
pancreas

gallbladder   **appendix**   **pancreas**

Complete each sentence.

Food passes from the **mouth** to the **pharynx** to the **esophagus** and then to the **stomach**, where gastric juices break up proteins and other molecules. From the stomach, food passes to the **small intestine** where nutrients are absorbed into the body's bloodstream. Undigested material moves into the **large intestine**, or colon, where water is resorbed and the residual material is compacted. This material, now known as feces, moves into the **rectum** where it is stored temporarily until it passes out of the **anus**. Above the stomach is the **liver**, and nested below the stomach is the **pancreas**, which secretes many of the digestive enzymes.

84

Answer Key

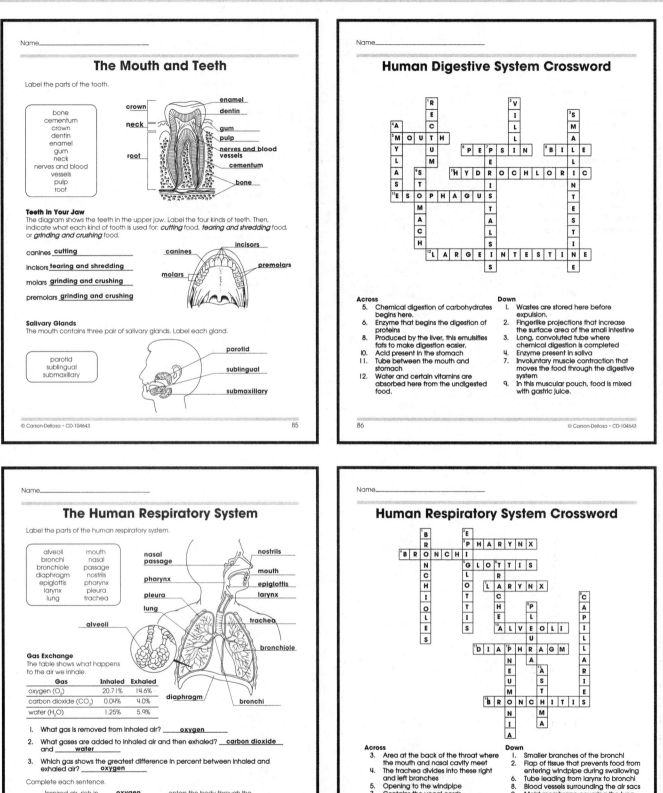

Name_____

The Mouth and Teeth

Label the parts of the tooth.

bone
cementum
crown
dentin
enamel
gum
neck
nerves and blood vessels
pulp
root

crown — enamel
neck — dentin
— gum
— pulp
root — nerves and blood vessels
— cementum
— bone

Teeth In Your Jaw
The diagram shows the teeth in the upper jaw. Label the four kinds of teeth. Then, indicate what each kind of tooth is used for: *cutting* food, *tearing and shredding* food, or *grinding and crushing* food.

canines __cutting__

incisors __tearing and shredding__

molars __grinding and crushing__

premolars __grinding and crushing__

incisors
canines
premolars
molars

Salivary Glands
The mouth contains three pair of salivary glands. Label each gland.

parotid
sublingual
submaxillary

parotid
sublingual
submaxillary

Name_____

Human Digestive System Crossword

Across
5. Chemical digestion of carbohydrates begins here.
6. Enzyme that begins the digestion of proteins
8. Produced by the liver, this emulsifies fats to make digestion easier.
10. Acid present in the stomach
11. Tube between the mouth and stomach
12. Water and certain vitamins are absorbed here from the undigested food.

Down
1. Wastes are stored here before expulsion.
2. Fingerlike projections that increase the surface area of the small intestine
3. Long, convoluted tube where chemical digestion is completed
4. Enzyme present in saliva
7. Involuntary muscle contraction that moves the food through the digestive system
9. In this muscular pouch, food is mixed with gastric juice.

Crossword answers: RECTUM, VILLI, SMALL INTESTINE, AMYLASE, MOUTH, PEPSIN, BILE, STOMACH, HYDROCHLORIC, ESOPHAGUS, PERISTALSIS, LARGE INTESTINE

Name_____

The Human Respiratory System

Label the parts of the human respiratory system.

alveoli   mouth
bronchi   nasal
bronchiole   passage
diaphragm   nostrils
epiglottis   pharynx
larynx   pleura
lung   trachea

nasal passage — nostrils
pharynx — mouth
pleura — epiglottis
lung — larynx
alveoli — trachea
— bronchiole
diaphragm — bronchi

Gas Exchange
The table shows what happens to the air we inhale.

Gas	Inhaled	Exhaled
oxygen (O_2)	20.71%	14.6%
carbon dioxide (CO_2)	0.04%	4.0%
water (H_2O)	1.25%	5.9%

1. What gas is removed from inhaled air? __oxygen__
2. What gases are added to inhaled air and then exhaled? __carbon dioxide__ and __water__
3. Which gas shows the greatest difference in percent between inhaled and exhaled air? __oxygen__

Complete each sentence.

Inspired air, rich in __oxygen__, enters the body through the __nostrils__, or __mouth__. It passes through the __pharynx__, and __larynx__, or voice box, and into the __trachea__. Air then enters each __bronchi__, which branches into __bronchioles__, and finally into the air sacs or __alveoli__ of the __lungs__. The lungs are housed in the __thoracic__ cavity that is bound on the bottom by a thin layer of muscle, the __diaphragm__. Each lung is covered by a very thin __pleural__ membrane. In the alveoli, __carbon dioxide__ is exchanged for oxygen.

Name_____

Human Respiratory System Crossword

Across
3. Area at the back of the throat where the mouth and nasal cavity meet
4. The trachea divides into these right and left branches
5. Opening to the windpipe
7. Contains the vocal cords
10. Tiny air sacs where the exchange of gases between air and blood takes place
11. Flat sheet of muscle separating the chest cavity from the abdominal cavity
14. Inflammation of the lining of the bronchial tubes

Down
1. Smaller branches of the bronchi
2. Flap of tissue that prevents food from entering windpipe during swallowing
6. Tube leading from larynx to bronchi
8. Blood vessels surrounding the air sacs
9. Moist membrane covering the lung and chest cavity wall on each side
12. Infection of the lungs caused by viruses, bacteria, or fungi
13. Bronchial spasm resulting in decreased air movement and air trapped in alveoli

Crossword answers: BRONCHIOLES, EPIGLOTTIS, PHARYNX, BRONCHI, GLOTTIS, TRACHEA, LARYNX, PNEUMONIA, PLEURA, ASTHMA, CAPILLARIES, ALVEOLI, DIAPHRAGM, BRONCHITIS

Answer Key

Panel 1

Name_____

The Human Urinary Tract and Kidney

Label the parts of the human urinary system. Give the function or purpose of each part.

kidney __remove excess liquid and other substances from blood__

adrenal glands __produce hormones__

ureter __joins kidney to bladder__

urinary bladder __stores urine until released from the body__

urethra __neck of bladder__

renal artery __artery leading to kidneys__

renal vein __vein coming from the kidneys__

cortex __outer portion of kidney__

medulla __inner portion of kidney__

renal pelvis __central area of kidney__

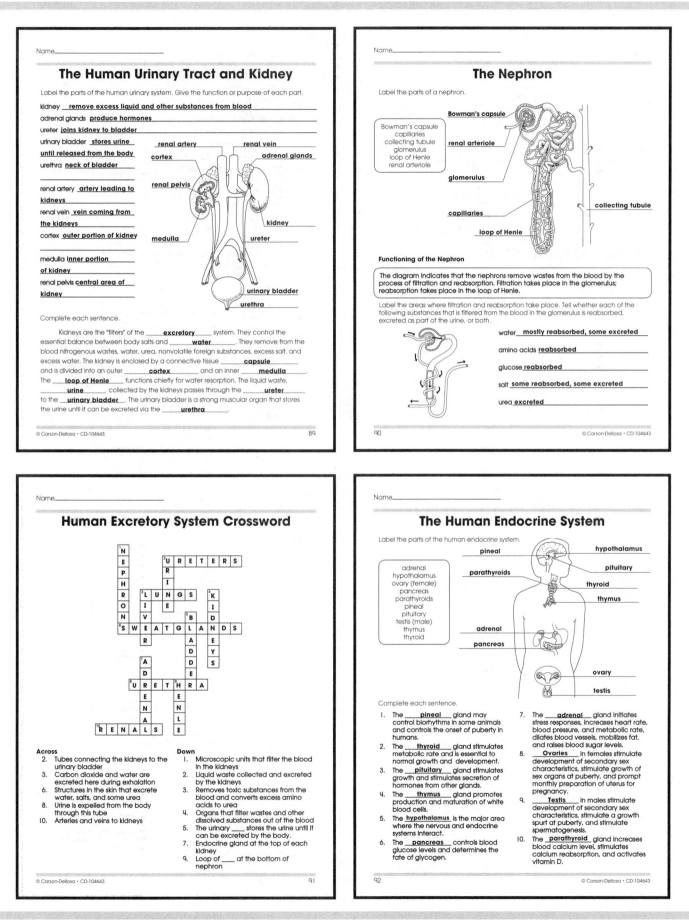

renal artery   renal vein
cortex   adrenal glands
renal pelvis
kidney
medulla   ureter
urinary bladder
urethra

Complete each sentence.

Kidneys are the "filters" of the ____excretory____ system. They control the essential balance between body salts and ____water____. They remove from the blood nitrogenous wastes, water, urea, nonvolatile foreign substances, excess salt, and excess water. The kidney is enclosed by a connective tissue ____capsule____ and is divided into an outer ____cortex____ and an inner ____medulla____. The ____loop of Henle____ functions chiefly for water resorption. The liquid waste, ____urine____, collected by the kidneys passes through the ____ureter____ to the ____urinary bladder____. The urinary bladder is a strong muscular organ that stores the urine until it can be excreted via the ____urethra____.

Panel 2

Name_____

The Nephron

Label the parts of a nephron.

Bowman's capsule
capillaries
collecting tubule
glomerulus
loop of Henle
renal arteriole

Bowman's capsule
renal arteriole
glomerulus
collecting tubule
capillaries
loop of Henle

Functioning of the Nephron

The diagram indicates that the nephrons remove wastes from the blood by the process of filtration and reabsorption. Filtration takes place in the glomerulus; reabsorption takes place in the loop of Henle.

Label the areas where filtration and reabsorption take place. Tell whether each of the following substances that is filtered from the blood in the glomerulus is reabsorbed, excreted as part of the urine, or both.

water __mostly reabsorbed, some excreted__

amino acids __reabsorbed__

glucose __reabsorbed__

salt __some reabsorbed, some excreted__

urea __excreted__

Panel 3

Name_____

Human Excretory System Crossword

Crossword grid:

1 across/down N-E-P-H-R-O-N-S
2 URETERS / RISE
3 LUNGS / LIVE
4 KIDNEYS
6 SWEATGLANDS
7 ADRENAL / BLADDER
8 URETHRA / KENLE
10 RENALS

Across
2. Tubes connecting the kidneys to the urinary bladder
3. Carbon dioxide and water are excreted here during exhalation
6. Structures in the skin that excrete water, salts, and some urea
8. Urine is expelled from the body through this tube
10. Arteries and veins to kidneys

Down
1. Microscopic units that filter the blood in the kidneys
2. Liquid waste collected and excreted by the kidneys
3. Removes toxic substances from the blood and converts excess amino acids to urea
4. Organs that filter wastes and other dissolved substances out of the blood
5. The urinary ____ stores the urine until it can be excreted by the body.
7. Endocrine gland at the top of each kidney
9. Loop of ____ at the bottom of nephron

Panel 4

Name_____

The Human Endocrine System

Label the parts of the human endocrine system.

adrenal
hypothalamus
ovary (female)
pancreas
parathyroids
pineal
pituitary
testis (male)
thymus
thyroid

pineal   hypothalamus
parathyroids   pituitary
thyroid
thymus
adrenal
pancreas
ovary
testis

Complete each sentence.

1. The ____pineal____ gland may control biorhythms in some animals and controls the onset of puberty in humans.
2. The ____thyroid____ gland stimulates metabolic rate and is essential to normal growth and development.
3. The ____pituitary____ gland stimulates growth and stimulates secretion of hormones from other glands.
4. The ____thymus____ gland promotes production and maturation of white blood cells.
5. The ____hypothalamus____ is the major area where the nervous and endocrine systems interact.
6. The ____pancreas____ controls blood glucose levels and determines the fate of glycogen.
7. The ____adrenal____ gland initiates stress responses, increases heart rate, blood pressure, and metabolic rate, dilates blood vessels, mobilizes fat, and raises blood sugar levels.
8. ____Ovaries____ in females stimulate development of secondary sex characteristics, stimulate growth of sex organs at puberty, and prompt monthly preparation of uterus for pregnancy.
9. ____Testis____ in males stimulate development of secondary sex characteristics, stimulate a growth spurt at puberty, and stimulate spermatogenesis.
10. The ____parathyroid____ gland increases blood calcium level, stimulates calcium reabsorption, and activates vitamin D.

Answer Key

Name_____

Human Hormones

The major hormones produced by the human body are:

ACTH	cortisol	insulin	prolactin
adrenaline	estrogen	Luteinizing hormone	testosterone
aldosterone	FSH	noradrenaline	thyroxin
calcitonin	glucagon	parathormone	TSH
	growth hormone	progesterone	

Next to each gland, write the name of the hormone or hormones it produces.

1. pituitary **ACTH, TSH, growth hormones, FSH, prolactin, Luteinizing hormone**
2. thyroid **thyroxin**
3. parathyroid **parathormone**
4. adrenal **cortisol, aldosterone, adrenaline, noradrenaline**
5. pancreas (islets of Langerhans) **insulin, glucagon**
6. testis **testosterone**
7. ovary **estrogen, progesterone**

Next to each function, write the name of the hormone that produces this effect.

8. raises the blood sugar level and increases the heartbeat and breathing rates — **adrenaline**
9. causes glucose to be removed from the blood and stored — **insulin**
10. influences the development of female secondary sex characteristics — **estrogen**
11. promotes the conversion of glycogen to glucose — **glucagon**
12. controls the metabolism of calcium — **parathormone**
13. promotes the reabsorption of sodium and potassium ions by the kidney — **aldosterone**
14. influences the development of male secondary sex characteristics — **testosterone**
15. stimulates the elongation of the long bones of the body — **growth hormone**
16. stimulates the secretion of hormones by the cortex of the adrenal glands — **ACTH**
17. regulates the rate of metabolism in the body — **thyroxin**
18. stimulates the development of eggs in the female's ovary — **FSH**
19. involved in the regulation of carbohydrate, protein, and fat metabolism — **cortisol**
20. stimulates the production of thyroxin — **TSH**

© Carson-Dellosa • CD-104643   93

Name_____

Structure of a Bird's Egg

Label the parts of the newly fertilized bird's egg and the developing bird's egg in the diagrams. Give the function or purpose of each part.

shell **thick outer covering of egg**
amnion **sac surrounding embryo**
amniotic fluid **protects embryo from injury and keeps it moist**
embryo **developing bird**
chorion **membrane surrounding embryo and yolk sac**
yolk sac **contains nutrients for developing bird**
blood vessels **lead to yolk sac from embryo**
allantois **carries out respiration and receives waste from embryo**
albumin **white portion of egg**
air space **area in flatter end of egg where gasses interchange**
shell membrane **thin layer just inside the shell**
yolk **yellow part of egg; source of food for developing embryo**
chalaza **twisted strands that suspend yolk and embryo in egg**

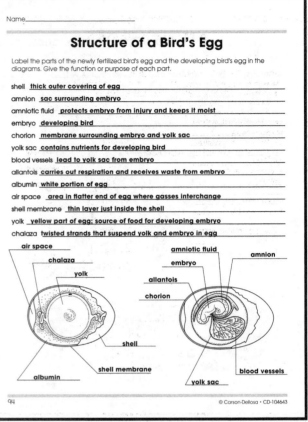

94   © Carson-Dellosa • CD-104643

Name_____

The Male Reproductive System

Label the parts of the male reproductive system.

Cowper's gland
epididymis
penis
prostate gland
scrotum
seminal vesicle
testis
urethra
urinary bladder
vas deferens

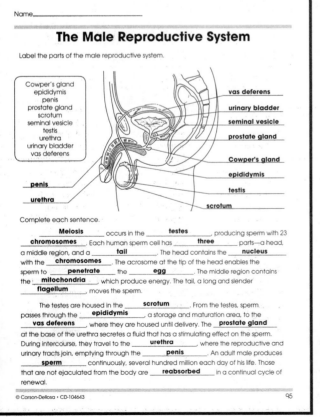

vas deferens
urinary bladder
seminal vesicle
prostate gland
Cowper's gland
epididymis
testis
scrotum
penis
urethra

Complete each sentence.

Meiosis occurs in the **testes**, producing sperm with 23 **chromosomes**. Each human sperm cell has **three** parts—a head, a middle region, and a **tail**. The head contains the **nucleus** with the **chromosomes**. The acrosome at the tip of the head enables the sperm to **penetrate** the **egg**. The middle region contains the **mitochondria**, which produce energy. The tail, a long and slender **flagellum**, moves the sperm.

The testes are housed in the **scrotum**. From the testes, sperm passes through the **epididymis**, a storage and maturation area, to the **vas deferens**, where they are housed until delivery. The **prostate gland** at the base of the urethra secretes a fluid that has a stimulating effect on the sperm. During intercourse, they travel to the **urethra**, where the reproductive and urinary tracts join, emptying through the **penis**. An adult male produces **sperm** continuously, several hundred million each day of his life. Those that are not ejaculated from the body are **reabsorbed** in a continual cycle of renewal.

© Carson-Dellosa • CD-104643   95

Name_____

The Female Reproductive System

Label the parts of the female reproductive system.

cervix
Fallopian tube
ovary
urethra
urinary bladder
uterus
vagina

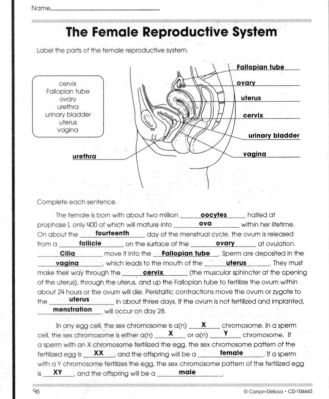

Fallopian tube
ovary
uterus
cervix
urinary bladder
vagina
urethra

Complete each sentence.

The female is born with about two million **oocytes** halted at prophase I, only 400 of which will mature into **ova** within her lifetime. On about the **fourteenth** day of the menstrual cycle, the ovum is released from a **follicle** on the surface of the **ovary** at ovulation. **Cilia** move it into the **Fallopian tube**. Sperm are deposited in the **vagina**, which leads to the mouth of the **uterus**. They must make their way through the **cervix** (the muscular sphincter at the opening of the uterus), through the uterus, and up the Fallopian tube to fertilize the ovum within about 24 hours or the ovum will die. Peristaltic contractions move the ovum or zygote to the **uterus** in about three days. If the ovum is not fertilized and implanted, **menstration** will occur on day 28.

In any egg cell, the sex chromosome is a(n) **X** chromosome. In a sperm cell, the sex chromosome is either a(n) **X** or a(n) **Y** chromosome. If a sperm with an X chromosome fertilized the egg, the sex chromosome pattern of the fertilized egg is **XX**, and the offspring will be a **female**. If a sperm with a Y chromosome fertilizes the egg, the sex chromosome pattern of the fertilized egg is **XY**, and the offspring will be a **male**.

96   © Carson-Dellosa • CD-104643

Answer Key

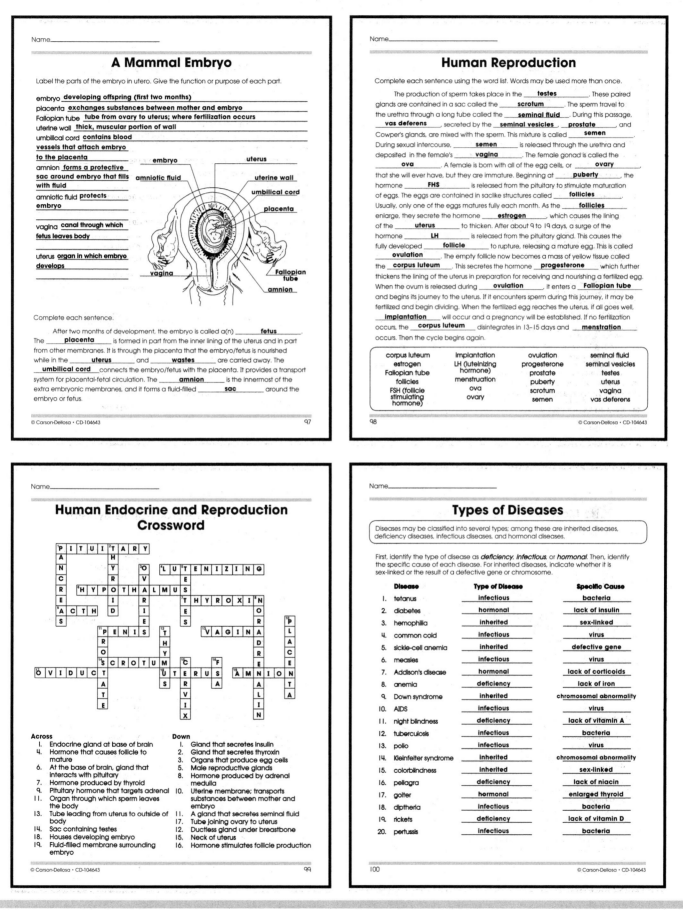

A Mammal Embryo

Label the parts of the embryo in utero. Give the function or purpose of each part.

embryo **developing offspring (first two months)**
placenta **exchanges substances between mother and embryo**
Fallopian tube **tube from ovary to uterus; where fertilization occurs**
uterine wall **thick, muscular portion of wall**
umbilical cord **contains blood vessels that attach embryo to the placenta**
amnion **forms a protective sac around embryo that fills with fluid**
amniotic fluid **protects embryo**
vagina **canal through which fetus leaves body**
uterus **organ in which embryo develops**

Labels on diagram: embryo, amniotic fluid, uterus, uterine wall, umbilical cord, placenta, vagina, Fallopian tube, amnion

Complete each sentence.

After two months of development, the embryo is called a(n) **fetus**. The **placenta** is formed in part from the inner lining of the uterus and in part from other membranes. It is through the placenta that the embryo/fetus is nourished while in the **uterus** and **wastes** are carried away. The **umbilical cord** connects the embryo/fetus with the placenta. It provides a transport system for placental-fetal circulation. The **amnion** is the innermost of the extra embryonic membranes, and it forms a fluid-filled **sac** around the embryo or fetus.

Human Reproduction

Complete each sentence using the word list. Words may be used more than once.

The production of sperm takes place in the **testes**. These paired glands are contained in a sac called the **scrotum**. The sperm travel to the urethra through a long tube called the **seminal fluid**. During this passage, **vas deferens**, secreted by the **seminal vesicles**, **prostate**, and Cowper's glands, are mixed with the sperm. This mixture is called **semen**. During sexual intercourse, **semen** is released through the urethra and deposited in the female's **vagina**. The female gonad is called the **ova**. A female is born with all of the egg cells, or **ovary**, that she will ever have, but they are immature. Beginning at **puberty**, the hormone **FHS** is released from the pituitary to stimulate maturation of eggs. The eggs are contained in saclike structures called **follicles**. Usually, only one of the eggs matures fully each month. As the **follicles** enlarge, they secrete the hormone **estrogen**, which causes the lining of the **uterus** to thicken. After about 9 to 19 days, a surge of the hormone **LH** is released from the pituitary gland. This causes the fully developed **follicle** to rupture, releasing a mature egg. This is called **ovulation**. The empty follicle now becomes a mass of yellow tissue called the **corpus luteum**. This secretes the hormone **progesterone** which further thickens the lining of the uterus in preparation for receiving and nourishing a fertilized egg. When the ovum is released during **ovulation**, it enters a **Fallopian tube** and begins its journey to the uterus. If it encounters sperm during this journey, it may be fertilized and begin dividing. When the fertilized egg reaches the uterus, if all goes well, **implantation** will occur and a pregnancy will be established. If no fertilization occurs, the **corpus luteum** disintegrates in 13–15 days and **menstration** occurs. Then the cycle begins again.

corpus luteum	Implantation	ovulation	seminal fluid
estrogen	LH (luteinizing hormone)	progesterone	seminal vesicles
Fallopian tube	menstruation	prostate	testes
follicles		puberty	uterus
FSH (follicle stimulating hormone)	ova	scrotum	vagina
	ovary	semen	vas deferens

Human Endocrine and Reproduction Crossword

Crossword answers:
P I T U I T A R Y
P A N C R E A S (down), T H Y R O I D (down), O V A R Y (down)
L U T E N I Z I N G (across)
H Y P O T H A L M U S (across)
T H Y R O X I N (across)
A C T H (across)
P E N I S (across), V A G I N A (across)
S C R O T U M (across), U T E R U S (across), A M N I O N (across)
O V I D U C T (across)
P R O S T A T E, C E R V I X, F S H, P L A C E N T A (down)

Across
1. Endocrine gland at base of brain
4. Hormone that causes follicle to mature
6. At the base of brain, gland that interacts with pituitary
7. Hormone produced by thyroid
9. Pituitary hormone that targets adrenal
11. Organ through which sperm leaves the body
13. Tube leading from uterus to outside of body
14. Sac containing testes
18. Houses developing embryo
19. Fluid-filled membrane surrounding embryo

Down
1. Gland that secretes insulin
2. Gland that secretes thyroxin
3. Organs that produce egg cells
5. Male reproductive glands
8. Hormone produced by adrenal medulla
10. Uterine membrane; transports substances between mother and embryo
11. A gland that secretes seminal fluid
17. Tube joining ovary to uterus
12. Ductless gland under breastbone
15. Neck of uterus
16. Hormone stimulates follicle production

Types of Diseases

Diseases may be classified into several types; among these are inherited diseases, deficiency diseases, infectious diseases, and hormonal diseases.

First, identify the type of disease as **deficiency**, **infectious**, or **hormonal**. Then, identify the specific cause of each disease. For inherited diseases, indicate whether it is sex-linked or the result of a defective gene or chromosome.

	Disease	Type of Disease	Specific Cause
1.	tetanus	infectious	bacteria
2.	diabetes	hormonal	lack of insulin
3.	hemophilia	inherited	sex-linked
4.	common cold	infectious	virus
5.	sickle-cell anemia	inherited	defective gene
6.	measles	infectious	virus
7.	Addison's disease	hormonal	lack of corticoids
8.	anemia	deficiency	lack of iron
9.	Down syndrome	inherited	chromosomal abnormality
10.	AIDS	infectious	virus
11.	night blindness	deficiency	lack of vitamin A
12.	tuberculosis	infectious	bacteria
13.	polio	infectious	virus
14.	Kleinfelter syndrome	inherited	chromosomal abnormality
15.	colorblindness	inherited	sex-linked
16.	pellagra	deficiency	lack of niacin
17.	goiter	hormonal	enlarged thyroid
18.	diptheria	infectious	bacteria
19.	rickets	deficiency	lack of vitamin D
20.	pertussis	infectious	bacteria

Answer Key

Name_____

Metamorphosis

As insects develop, they undergo **metamorphosis**, a series of definite changes in appearance. Some insects, such as a butterfly, undergo complete metamorphosis. Other insects, such as the grasshopper, undergo incomplete metamorphosis.

Label the stages on the diagram of the complete metamorphosis of the butterfly and incomplete metamorphosis of the grasshopper.

Complete Metamorphosis   **Incomplete Metamorphosis**

egg — larva — pupa — adult   egg — nymph — adult

Complete each sentence.

In complete metamorphosis, a female butterfly hatches into a wormlike organism called a **larva**, or caterpillar. During this stage, the organism consumes a large amount of food. The **larva**, or caterpillar, then spins a protective covering around itself and becomes a(n) **pupa**, or chrysalis. This covering is called a **cocoon**. While inside this covering, the **pupa** changes into a(n) **adult**.

In **incomplete** metamorphosis, a grasshopper goes through a(n) **gradual** change from egg to **adult**. The grasshopper begins as a(n) **egg** and hatches into a(n) **nymph**. A nymph is an immature **grasshopper** that resembles a full-grown grasshopper but lacks **wings**. As the nymph grows, it **molts** until it reaches the last stage, the **adult**.

Name_____

Evolution

Five evidences of evolution are fossil evidence (*a*), homologous structures (*b*), embryology (*c*), vestigial organs (*d*), and biochemical (*e*). Write the letter of the type of evidence by each example.

b 1. Bones in a bird's wing and a human's arm are similar in structure.

e 2. All organisms use ATP in energy transfers.

c 3. There are similarities in structure among the early stages of fish, birds, and humans.

d 4. Humans, unlike rabbits, have no known use for their appendix.

a 5. Horses have increased in size and decreased in number of toes since the Eocene.

Match the terms with the correct definition or name.

c 1. genetic drift
d 2. gradualism
e 3. natural selection
j 4. divergent evolution
b 5. punctuated equilibrium
i 6. mass extinction
g 7. mutations
a 8. gene pool
k 9. convergent evolution
f 10. radioactive dating
h 11. use and disuse

a. all genes in a population
b. brief periods of change interrupt long stable periods
c. changes in gene frequency in small populations
d. changes occur gradually over time
e. Darwin
f. determing age of fossils
g. gene or chromosomal changes
h. Lamarck
i. many species vanish at one time
j. unrelated species become less alike
k. unrelated species become more alike

Number the steps of Darwin's Theory of Evolution in order.

2 Struggle for Existence   **4** Natural Selection

1 Overproduction   **3** Variation